Don't Just Teach: Be a Teacher

Don't Just Teach: Be a Teacher

What It Means to Exercise the Gift of Teaching in the Church

JOHN RUE DAVIS

RESOURCE *Publications* · Eugene, Oregon

DON'T JUST TEACH: BE A TEACHER
What It Means to Exercise the Gift of Teaching in the Church

Resource Publications
An Imprint of Wipf and Stock Publishers
199 W. 8th Ave., Suite 3
Eugene, OR 97401

www.wipfandstock.com

PAPERBACK ISBN: 978-1-5326-7660-4
HARDCOVER ISBN: 978-1-5326-7661-1
EBOOK ISBN: 978-1-5326-7662-8

Manufactured in the U.S.A.   APRIL 1, 2019

Dedicated to my wonderful wife of forty years who has read the entire manuscript multiple times and has served with me in training ministers and local church workers.

Contents

Preface

MOST CHURCHES TODAY HAVE that a purpose statement or similar document. Virtually all of these statements have "edify" or a similar term listed as one of its objectives. In some cases whole denominations such as the Assemblies of God has "edifying of the body of Christ" written into its doctrinal statement on the mission of the church. The way local churches work out this edifying of the body varies from church to church and a wide variety of activities have been included. However, nearly every one of these approaches to edifying has two things in common; working in subgroups of the church and some form of teaching.

Teaching happens at some point in nearly every subgroup of the church. Often it is the main focus as in adult education or Sunday school classes. However, when children's activities take place from Awana's to children's church teaching plays a role in the meeting. When the men's or women's fellowship groups gather there is usually some kind of teaching activity. While the teenagers may go to theme parks on some occasions, there are certainly plenty of others when they are taught about something. On mid-week meeting nights teaching happens in nearly every group that meets. The resulting quantity of teaching that believers are exposed to in the church can be quite large if they attend several different groups. For instance if a believer attends Sunday school and a separate adult fellowship they could easily sit through more than an hour of teaching in any given week. If they are also involved in some other activity whether with children or the ladies fellowship the quantity of teaching rises even more.

In the majority of cases, this teaching is done by untrained laypersons. Pastors are limited to being in one place at a time. When multiple groups meet simultaneously the most a pastor can do is to be one of the teachers or travel from room to room to observe. While pastors may address the whole church on Sundays most preach less than an hour. Yet, many in the church attend multiple groups all of which include teaching. As a result, they receive more instruction from untrained lay people than from trained pastors. Put another way the church is filled with people with no particular training who carry out the majority of its teaching function.

A different way to view this situation is that many in the church as a part of their service to the Lord are called on to be teachers. Sometimes they are called upon to do this with no training at all. Everyone has heard the horror story of the new believer given a teacher's guide and sent into the junior boys' class. More often people called on to teach have at least had the experience of listening to other's teaching. This gives them at a minimum an example as a basis for their own efforts. In the best cases, they have been to some seminar or occasionally a class for teachers. These types of training have typically emphasized techniques for presenting material. What is usually left out is what it means to be a teacher. There is a huge difference between filling the role of a teacher and realizing that you are being used by God as a teacher. This book is largely addressed to people who as part of their service to the Lord are called on to be teachers. It is dedicated to the idea that they should recognize that they are not merely filling a slot but are called by God to be teachers and not merely people who happen to teach.

1

Teaching as a Ministry
in the Church

WHEN JESUS SENT OUT his disciples into all the world He specifically told them that they were to teach.

> 18 Then Jesus came to them and said, "All authority in heaven and on earth has been given to me. 19 Therefore go and make disciples of all nations, baptizing them in the name of the Father and of the Son and of the Holy Spirit, 20 and teaching them to obey everything I have commanded you. And surely I am with you always, to the very end of the age." Matt 28:18–20 (NIV)

This mirrors Jesus' own ministry. In the Gospels Jesus is referred to as Teacher or a teacher over forty times according to the NIV. In contrast, He is said to preach only five times. While this is a somewhat arbitrary distinction, it clearly shows that teaching was a major part of His ministry. While we rightly think of preaching when we speak of the great commission, clearly part of fulfilling the great commission requires teaching those who are converted.

This is seen in the book of Acts: the first church met daily at the Temple with part of these meetings devoted to the apostles' teaching. Later in Acts 5:42, the apostles are also mentioned as teaching from house to house. When the believers are scattered in the persecution that followed Stephen's martyrdom, we are told that those scattered preached where ever they went. In following what they knew of the Lord's own practice and the apostles' practice, these scattered evangelists would have not only preached salvation but also taught their new converts the details of what they themselves knew about the Lord.

As the Church expanded, what started as forced scattering and informal missionary effort began to be organized. Over the next few years as the church reached farther and farther from Jerusalem and the original apostles, it was forced to think again about organization and leadership. In Antioch of Syria, the church started by these informal missionaries grew to have leaders designated as 'prophets and teachers'. After about a year, and lead by the Holy Spirit, Paul and Barnabas were sent out as the first intentional missionaries.[1] This leads to a tremendous expansion in the number of believers and church locations.

Remember, the core of church leadership is still dominantly Jewish. They have the benefit of generations of experience in serving God as a minority scattered across the world. Just as the Jews who were dispersed across the world organized themselves in synagogues, Barnabas and Paul follow the same pattern by creating local fellowships of believers. In addition, following the synagogue pattern, local leadership is clearly required for these believers to continue in the Faith. Led by the Holy Spirit and beginning in their first mission's trip Barnabas and Paul leave behind elders in each church. Paul later, in the Pastoral Epistles, lays out instructions for selecting local leadership in the form of elders and deacons.

As the church continues to grow, the Holy Spirit reveals that every believer has some part to play in the Lord's service. Paul develops this as a formal teaching in 1 Corinthians by describing believers as parts of Christ's body. "Now you are the body of Christ, and each one of you is a part of it." 1 Cor. 12:27 NIV He explains that just as the parts of the body have different functions all of

---

1. Acts 13:1

which are important, so do believers. Paul is clear that everyone has some function and they should be fulfilling that function.

The importance of the idea that everyone has a function in the church cannot be overemphasized. The functions vary greatly, but all are needed and complimentary to each other. Again, since the church is like a person's body, it is fair to ask how we view a body that has parts that are not functioning normally. The answer is that the body is sick and needs to be made well. Various treatments are applied to try to help the whole body to function properly again. If a person has some parts actually missing they are usually described as handicapped. At that point people will look for some artificial way to restore the missing functionality. Bodies are designed by God to have all their parts present and functional.

In Romans 12 Paul expands the picture of the church as a body by describing how different parts function. Paul, led by the Spirit, describes these functions of the church body in terms of specific kinds of service. He teaches that each kind of service is a gift from God working in an individual believer. He lists seven examples of how people are gifted to serve in the body of Christ.

> 3 For by the grace given me I say to every one of you:
> Do not think of yourself more highly than you ought,
> but rather think of yourself with sober judgment, in ac-
> cordance with the measure of faith God has given you.
> 4 Just as each of us has one body with many members,
> and these members do not all have the same function, 5
> so in Christ we who are many form one body, and each
> member belongs to all the others. 6 We have different
> gifts, according to the grace given us. If a man's gift is
> prophesying, let him use it in proportion to his faith. 7 If
> it is serving, let him serve; if it is teaching, let him teach;
> 8 if it is encouraging, let him encourage; if it is contribut-
> ing to the needs of others, let him give generously; if it
> is leadership, let him govern diligently; if it is showing
> mercy, let him do it cheerfully. Rom 12:3–8 NIV

Notice how this list of prophecy, serving, teaching, encouraging, giving, leadership, governing, and showing mercy is centered on working with people not technology. For example, there are no listings for blacksmiths, potters, sailors, hunters, herdsmen, or farmers though these positions existed all around the church. Rather every form of service Paul mentions involves people working with people and can be applied in any and every culture. Whether a church is located in first century Corinth, in twentieth century Manhattan, or in a rainforest it needs prophets, those who serve, teachers, encouragers, givers, leaders, and those who show mercy. Any church lacking in any of these functions would soon find itself wanting that function.

Further, it is important to understand that God has not left His church dependent upon the merely human talents of those who respond to the Gospel message. Instead, God Himself has gifted individual believers to provide the church with the necessary functions. Because these functions are gifts from God it means that the work of God can be done not in human strength but in the power that God provides. These gifts, on any occasion, align with natural talent but often they are exercised through individuals who in the natural would not be inclined to the function at all.

While these functions may overlap the offices or gifts of Christ to the church listed in Ephesians 4:11–12, in activity, these gifts are given to all the members of the body and not just those called to formal and often full-time service. These functions are gifts that involve everyone who is part of the body of Christ. Not only so, but the functions listed are just what any organization needs for smooth operation. In any organization, someone must count the money, someone must keep track of people, someone must provide service, and someone must organize it all. The church, however, is far more than just another organization; it is the body of Christ. As such, it includes specific functions that are required to fulfill God's purpose. The result is that there are some who are gifted to prophesy, to show mercy, and to the current focus – those who are gifted by God to teach.

This book is focused on these teachers. It is not aimed at those called as teachers and pastors by Christ to offices in the church as in Ephesians 4:11. Rather, it is focused on those who while living for God and serving in the church find themselves with the gift of teaching as a part of their functioning in the body of Christ. Those who are called to the office of teacher and pastor are expected to teach as part of 'their ministry'. Most local church teachers hold no ministry office but receive the gift of teaching as part of their service. Frequently, they themselves do not even think of themselves as teachers. They just do a lesson with such and such a group. However, as was mentioned in the introduction, collectively they provide most of the church's teaching.

Those who teach the adults are often recognized for this teaching gift. After all, adults are important. However, everyone who is teaching is filling an important function and exercising a gift from God. This includes not only those who teach adults and youth but also those who teach children. The last group is often down-played as teachers. How much can you teach a five year old or an eight year old about deep spiritual truths? Surely anyone can do this. However, the church must not count their service to Christ as of little value or ignore their gift of teaching. To do so is to demean a gift God Himself has given the church. This is unwise and ultimately sinful.

The correct approach is to recognize and affirm the critical work done by all these teachers. The church must not and dare not ignore their work or count it of little value. We must never say she only teaches the second graders. Consider who actually communicates to these children the truths of the faith. Who answers the questions they have? Never forget the tremendous value Jesus set on children, rebuking the apostles who put adults first.[2] He even warned that those who hindered children would be better off dead.[3]

According to George Barna, thirty-two percent of children between five and twelve presented with the Gospel will accept the message. The same is true for only four percent of teenagers and six percent for all the rest of adulthood.[4] Based on this, those who teach children are likely to have the greatest direct impact on the

2. Mark 10:14

3. Matt 18:5–6

4. Barna, Transforming Children into Spiritual Champions, p. 41.

number of souls added to God's Kingdom of anyone working in the church. Understanding this ought to move us to honor and respect those teaching children. At the same time it should warn those entrusted with teaching children that as they accept this work from God as the weightiest of responsibilities.

The value of teaching children has a personal significance for me as my wife accepted Christ in a Sunday school class at the age of seven. She had been taken to Sunday school by her older sister for several weeks and then had left after the class and walked home by herself ahead of the worship service. She never heard the pastor preach. Her Sunday school teacher however, was alert to her situation and led her to Christ just after the class ended. That Sunday she stayed for worship and has served God ever since. If that teacher had not been personally interested in my wife and if the teacher had not been willing to stay a little late, my wife might not have become a Christian.

Beyond children, who helps new converts learn more than surface information about the Lord? Who provides specific instruction to the subgroups of the church like the men, women, new mothers, or older adults? Believing teenagers must work out how to live for God through the greatest period of change that they will experience. Pastors rarely have time to address detailed specific issues for any group. They provide general messages to the entire church. It is the teachers of these and other subgroups who apply the Word of God to the detailed issues of life. Teachers pass on to believers the 'everything I have commanded you' of Jesus' commission. Without the teachers of these small groups, the church believers would remain immature and unable to fulfill the work God has given them to do.

Another way to gage the great value of teachers is the amount of time they can be face to face with their students. Often the teacher of a group will have an hour a week to teach a lesson. The pastor rarely preaches over 45 minutes. In addition, the teacher will have many fewer listeners than the pastor and can focus much more on individuals. They generally interact in two-way verbal communication while teaching. Students will ask questions and answer questions from the teacher. Imagine a pastor halting the sermon to take questions. This is not to devalue pastors. It is rather to show the value of a different part of the Body of Christ which is sometimes not seen for the vital function it fulfills.

The point of all of this is that these teachers fulfill the majority of the teaching function of the Church. By working with small groups, these teachers do what pastors cannot do because of the limits of time and space. They fulfill a critical role in disciplining believers by teaching person to person the details of the faith. God has planned for this by giving the gift of teaching to these teachers so that they can be effective in this work not in their own ability but in the power that He gives. The church should therefore recognize these teachers as filling this position and their value in fulfilling the great commission. These teachers should also recognize themselves as teachers and take their gifting as teachers with the utmost seriousness as a sacred trust from God.

DISCUSSION QUESTIONS

1. Why are there teachers in the Church?
2. How does the expansion of the Church relate to the presence of lay teachers?
3. Why are lay teachers so important?
4. Why does it matter that teachers are a gift from God to the Church?
5. What makes teachers of children so important?

2

You Teach What You Are

"... everyone who is fully trained will be like his teacher."
—LUKE 6:40 NIV

STUDENTS NATURALLY ABSORB PART of their teacher. It is literally the nature of teaching that teachers transform students. If students are willing to receive the training that the teacher provides, they will become like their teacher in at least that area. Jesus expected his disciples to become like him as they listened and spent time with him. Consequently, those who teach ought to become the best teachers that they can become. This includes their working knowledge of the material taught and of their applied teaching techniques. Because they are teaching about the Lord, the character of teachers is especially important. Jesus said, "Everyone who is fully trained will be like his teacher." Luke 6:40 NIV This means teachers not only convey information but their very selves as believers in the form of their character. Teachers reproduce their character in their students.

It is common to speak about parents and condemn the attitude of those who tell their children to 'do as I say not as I do'.

This criticism is equally true for teachers. Students will even, if unconsciously, imitate their teacher. If you do or fail to do something, this will speak to your students far louder than any admonition that you give them in a class. Actions always influence more than words. Initially your students may not know about some parts of your life. Over time however, they will find out all about your life. You are in the same church. They will sit and eat with you at church dinners. They will know when you are sick or have some crisis. They will meet your spouse and family. If you are single in a healthy church they will invite you to some kinds of activities. Never doubt that over time your students will find out who you are and how you live. Your character as shown through your life will be observed and will have influence.

Your response to this may be 'I am only one teacher' there are many influences. This is true; but, you will be a part, and for some, you will be the most important part. Anyone who has gone through school will look back on favorite teachers—that is, on teachers who influenced who that student is today. At the time you were in school, the teacher or teachers you now remember were sometimes not the most liked or even respected. However, for some reason, over time they wielded significant influence in your life. This influence may have been for good or evil; but, it is real and changed who you are now. Because you are a teacher, you will be 'that teacher', for someone. You will be the one who changes someone's life. You will be the one who influences his life for good or evil.

Teachers rarely have the same level of influence as a pastor. However looking at the influence of a pastor can help you see the importance of this influence. In the best sense, a pastor teaches people the value of a godly life by living it in front of them. While you may not know all about his prayers, you will learn over time whether or not he spends much time alone with God. You discover if the pastor spends time in careful study of God's Word. You learn if the pastor treats his family well. Then, consciously or unconsciously, you are changed by that knowledge. Likewise, if the pastor is proud and sure of his own abilities you will realize it. If he emphasizes importance over service and is slack when it comes to prayer and study, it will come out over time.

In the best cases, people will grow in their own lives following the good example. They will learn what being a disciple of the Lord Jesus all is about and they will grow in their own walk. If the pastor makes time for those in need, the people will also. The congregation will turn to God in prayer when they are in need because they have seen the pastor relying upon prayer in his life. Good pastors lead people closer to God. In the worst-case scenario, if the pastor has some kind of moral failure, not just the church but the whole community will be affected. It does not matter whether the failure involves money, drugs, alcohol, or sex. People will be impacted. Some people will turn away from God. Some who might have been saved will never come to God. Everyone in contact, even indirectly, with the failure will have their life shaken to some degree.

As a teacher, you are unlikely to be as significant an influence on as broad a group of people as the pastor. Nevertheless, because of the direct small group interaction that is typical of most church teaching situations, your influence may actually be deeper and stronger on those whom you teach than that of the pastor. Most pastors have something of an inner circle, people they spend more time with than the average person in the congregation. This is not wrong. Jesus selected twelve "to be with Him". Even within the twelve Jesus had three He spent even more time with than the rest of the twelve. No pastor can have a deep close personal relationship with everyone in the congregation. No pastor can have deep discussions about truth with each of your students weekly, especially one on one and face to face. Conversely, you as the teacher can have those discussions. As a result, teachers often have more and deeper influence on their students than the pastor simply by being the one who is close and accessible weekly. Your student is more likely to ask you, the teacher, not the pastor, to pray about a situation at school or work. People will open up their lives in the small circle you influence in a way they will not to the pastor and cannot before the church as a whole. There is not enough time in a service for that to happen for everyone or enough hours in a day for the pastor to listen to all your students and pray with each of your students the way you as their teacher can listen and pray.

This means you will have influence on your students. Ultimately a great deal of that influence will come out in their imitation of your character. They will figure out if you really care about them or only enjoy being a teacher. They will quickly realize if you embrace or simply endure the job of teaching. They will figure out what your walk with God is like. They will know if you are real or a phony. You are responsible to God for what they find out and how it changes them.

The second great area of influence you have on your students is in what they believe to be true. This is especially true of younger students. When you tell a child something about God they are generally going to believe you. When you tell them that the Bible says something, then for them, that is what the Bible says. You are their truth filter. As a result, you must take care in what you say about God and His Word.

I once listened to a pastor describe walking past a Sunday school classroom and hearing a teacher tell an unruly child that, "Jesus doesn't love you when you are bad". The pastor recalls immediately taking the teacher into the hallway and telling her, "Don't you ever tell a child that Jesus doesn't love them!" The teacher obviously needed help with discipline in her classroom but her frustration caused her to tell a dangerous lie. Romans 5:8 says, "But God demonstrates his own love for us in this: While we were still sinners, Christ died for us." NIV To tell anyone for any reason that God does not love them when they sin is to cut them off from any hope of salvation. The teacher may not have meant to do this when she spoke, but it is what she said and the child is likely to remember the point.

As a pastor and now a Bible college professor I have heard many, many times 'I once heard a teacher or pastor say . . . Then they would assert something that could range from a wrong cultural understanding of a passage to complete heresy. They were not making up situations or statements. Some statement had been made and that statement had stuck in their minds. They still remembered it years later and in some cases had their thinking shaped by the statement. The danger is twofold: first that people will have wrong understandings about God and second the more subtle danger that if the falsehood is discovered everything you have said will come into question.

Two of the more innocuous examples involve the scourging of Jesus being with thirty-nine lashes and second, Jesus teaching about a camel going through the 'eye of the needle'. The first of these is based on a sloppy reading of the New Testament and a detailed knowledge of the Old Testament. In the Law God limits the severity of a judicially applied beating to forty strokes. By New Testament times, the legal limit of forty lashes was normally shortened to thirty-nine lest a miscount result in a violation of the Law by the court. This limit of thirty-nine strokes is then applied to scourging that Jesus received at His trial under Pilate. This is sometimes expanded by the assertion that there are thirty-nine different categories of sickness and that Jesus took one lash for each so that we could be healed. However, the entire line of reasoning is wrong because Jesus was not scourged by the Jews, but by the Romans. The Romans had no concern about the number of lashes. They simply beat to the point that to continue would result in immediate death. This is much more severe than what is allowed under the Old Testament Law.

The second example concerns what Jesus meant about a camel going through the eye of a needle. Matthew, Mark, and Luke all say, "it is easier for a camel to go through the eye of a needle than for a rich man to enter the kingdom of God" Matt 19:24, Mark 10:25, Luke 18:25 NIV. In each, this is immediately followed by the disciples' incredulous response of "who then can be saved?" They obviously understand the idea as, since a camel cannot possibly fit through the eye of a needle neither the rich, who they see as favored by God, nor anyone else can be saved. Jesus agrees with this but tells them, "that all things are possible with God". Some commentators having heard of a small door in the main gate of Jerusalem called "the eye of the needle" have identified this with Jesus' saying. They explain that for a camel to pass through this gate within a gate it must first get down on its knees and have its load of goods removed. From this they explain the meaning is that the rich must humble themselves and release the grip wealth burdens them with to be saved. The biggest problem with this explanation is that such gates were not used until centuries after the time of Christ. Theologically the effect is to make the way of salvation more natural when Jesus said salvation required a supernatural act of God.

While neither of these examples is likely to keep someone from heaven, they both are wrong understandings of God's Word. The second may even somewhat twist what is required for salvation. Perhaps more importantly is that today we deal with more skeptical students who have instant access to the internet. Even children in the primary grades may check our content by googling. We dare not be careless about an explanation of lessor matters if we wish to be wholly believed in the great matters of the nature of God and salvation.

The solution to false information is usually found in carefully preparing for a class. Studying the topic or passage beforehand will help to eliminate unintended statements that may be simply wrong. Working hard to grow in the knowledge of God's Word will also help prevent many erroneous statements. Learning how to evaluate a particular bit of information from a particular source comes with experience. It is also OK to say I do not know. This is far better than making a false statement. Anyone who teaches very much cannot and will not always be correct in everything they say. What we as teachers must strive to do is make as few wrong statements as possible and when we discover an error be willing to repair it if possible.

The third area of concern is that of teaching techniques. The importance of technique is less obvious than the first two areas. It is blatantly obvious that the content of teaching matters. It is also fairly easy to understand that when teaching Christianity that the character of the teacher matters. The reason how you teach also matters is that you are influencing the next wave of teachers. The way you teach will influence your students in how they should someday teach. Teachers learn to teach by watching others teach. What you use or fail to use as teaching techniques your students in turn will imitate when some of them are called of God as teachers.

This book is not about teaching techniques and which to choose for a given situation. However, when some of your students are gifted by God as teachers to the church they will to some extent follow your example. If you always teach by class discussion they will see leading a discussion as the sum total of teaching. If you always lecture they will see lecture as the whole of teaching. If all you do with children is have them color pictures, when as adults some of them are charged with teaching children, they will likely do the same.

The point is simply that the act of teaching, teaches how to teach. You are training some whom God will gift as teachers in the future. Because of this you must with God's help make the best conscious and intentional choices that you can in how you teach. Success will produce better teaching for all your current students and better prepare tomorrow's teachers. Failure will not only hurt those you are now teaching but will injure the next generation as well.

As a teacher you influence your students by everything you say, everything you are, and everything you do. Your character will make the facts you teach believable or call into question the reality of the Faith. Especially for children, it will establish what a mature Christian is like. The information you provide, the content of what you teach will be the basis of what your students believe about God. This is an awesome responsibility; teachers are the gate keepers of truth for the church. Finally, how you teach will either help future teachers excel or dull them. Your approach to the classroom will influence what they do long into the future.

DISCUSSION QUESTIONS

1. How does the teacher's character influence students?

2. How do students find out about a teacher's character?

3. Compare a teacher's influence to that of a pastor.

4. Why is the accuracy of what a teacher says about the Bible so important?

5. What are the most important ways that a teacher's influence extends into the future?

3

A Teacher Cares about Students

A TEACHER CARES ABOUT his students. His purpose is to help students to succeed in life. This attitude of the heart is the difference between someone who just presents information and someone who is truly a teacher. The idea is not unlike the difference between a leader who has a true pastor's heart and one who is simply a hireling. It is the difference between a pastor who cares deeply about those under him and a professional who fills a position without truly caring about those under him. A real teacher cares deeply about those who are in the position of being students, especially his students.

Perhaps the easiest way to show what makes a real teacher is to show what real teachers are not. In the world, the ultimate designation for a teacher is professor. Yet anyone with much college experience knows that professors can be haughty, distant, and completely unconcerned about students. Others have the designation of lecturer and that is exactly what they do. They lecture on a given topic. What people do with that material is entirely up to those who hear the lecturer. Some of those with these titles are teachers. Others are simply clock punchers and care nothing about those who are designated as their students. The key difference is whether or not they have a heart for those who hear them.

The focus of this book is mostly on volunteers. Since no paycheck is involved, they have little or no motive to fill the position of a teacher with the attitude of a clock puncher. This however does not automatically mean they have a teacher's heart. Some have simply been maneuvered into the job because the church needed someone to fill a slot. Often these people have accepted a position out of guilt. Others see a need that 'must' be met. Their gift may not be teaching, but, teaching must be done and teaching they will do. These are not bad people; but, they are not teachers! Some, however, who remain in the job will become teachers.

Another group that may readily volunteer is those who have been moved by a great teacher and who have a recording of that teacher. They have been helped by this teacher and they want others to also be helped as well. These come with good motives and share what has helped them that others may also be helped. These people are perhaps best described as facilitators. They are not teachers but they bring teachers to others. The weakness is that the actual teacher has no interaction with the students. They appear merely as a recording and therefore cannot care about individual students. Because they will never meet those who hear them they cannot adapt to student needs or answer questions. While the recorded teacher may have the heart of a teacher, because they appear only as a recording they function in the same way as an uncaring lecturer.

A good way to understand the relationship a teacher should have with students is to look to our master teacher, the Lord Jesus, and his relationship to Peter. Jesus built a relationship with Peter over time. He is first introduced to Peter by Andrew, Peter's brother, and spends time with Peter including going together to a wedding.[1] Later after teaching at Peter's synagogue, Jesus spent time in Peter's home and with his family.[2] When Jesus actually calls Peter, the call is personalized with a great catch of fish to show that Peter's material needs will be met and with a personalized phrase

1. John 1:40–42 , 2:2
2. Luke 4:38–39

"fishers of men".[3] At the last supper Jesus warns Peter that "he will be shifted like wheat" but, "I have prayed for you that your faith will not fail".[4] Peter is not a seat number, but a person Jesus, the teacher, knows and cares about.

This very brief retelling of the relationship Jesus built with Peter shows the individual care Jesus afforded to his students. He did not merely meet them for class, he knew them. Jesus took time to know about Peter's family and his work. People will object that this is fine for Jesus; but, who has the time! I have too many students to do it that way. It is true that even good teachers cannot visit every home for a meal let alone get to know the whole family. However, most volunteer teachers have fewer than a dozen regular students. Building personal relationships with students was important enough for Jesus to invest a significant amount of his very limited 3 years of ministry. In the same way, it should be important enough for the real teachers today to make real efforts to do the same.

Paul spent three years in Ephesus largely in teaching mode and holding classes daily. In Acts, Luke describes Paul's intense concern for his students and his tears over them.[5] Paul not only met with them at the lecture hall but also house to house.[6] Plainly, this was not a professional relationship with clearly and carefully delineated lines and limits. Rather, it was intensely personal. Later, when Paul departs for Jerusalem, we see the students in tears and terribly distressed.[7] When Paul later writes to the Ephesians he prays not once but twice over them.[8] He also requests their prayers for him in his present difficult circumstances that he will have enough courage to speak as he should.[9] Admitting that kind of weakness suggests that Paul had established a very personal

3. Luke 5:1–11

4. Luke 22:31–32

5. Acts 20:19

6. Acts 20:20

7. Acts 20:37–38

8. Ephesians 1:16–22, 3:16–20

9. Ephesians 6:19–20

kind of relationship with the Ephesians. Distant professionals generally do not admit to students that they may fail at the very thing that they teach.

Altogether, Paul's example of how he interacted with his students is similar to that of Jesus. Both built intensely personal relationships with their students. These relationships involved not just professional interactions but knowledge of family and home life. These were true two-way relationships. That is, concern flowed both from Jesus and Paul to the students and from the students to Jesus and Paul. Perhaps, most of all, the relationships involved prayer for the students. Admittedly, this sets a high standard for teachers today to follow. However, we are not trying to teach math or history but a walk with God Almighty.

The reason that a teacher must have a real relationship with his students that involves interaction is that Christianity is 'caught not taught'. Modeling of what is being taught is vital to the behavioral learning process. It is exceedingly difficult to model behavior for someone with whom you have little or no relationship. Remember, the goal of teaching in a church should never be simply knowledge gained; but rather, it should be knowledge that is applied in the lives of the students. It can be very hard to facilitate that kind of learning if the teacher has little or no knowledge about the students. For example, telling students that they should spend some time alone in their room everyday with God reading the Bible and praying is a poor instruction if they sleep on the sofa in the front room. What you teach must fit into the lives of your students and the only way you can know if that is happening is to know them. The only way they will follow your teaching is if you have genuine credibility in your relationship with them.

It is very hard to build a relationship with someone you know little or nothing about. Teachers therefore need to find ways to gain some knowledge of their students in order to have a meaningful relationship so that they can teach not just facts but Christian behavior. Gaining this kind of information is not unachievable or even extremely difficult. A good first step is simply paying attention to what is said during informal contacts before and after class.

This is a nonthreatening method that will provide much of the needed information. Asking adults casual questions about the wife or husband, children, and job may yield useful information about the student. Asking children about favorite activities, programs, games, and family may be very revealing. These and other carefully worded questions and careful attention to the answers can reveal much about the relationships a student experiences within his family. For adults and children, providing occasions for social interaction can greatly expand the possibilities for asking these sorts of questions.

Sometimes a coffee break is the most important part of a class. In the ministry preparation classes that my wife and I teach, we often include a break halfway through for people to stand up and take a breather. We make sure there is something to drink and often some small snack. We can ask in these casual times about how things are going at work or how a class they are teaching is doing. The most important questions we are asked in any given class often come before the class starts, after it is officially over, or during these breaks. If students are trying to apply the Gospel in their lives, they are often uncomfortable speaking about it in front of the whole class. People are people and they frequently fear looking weak or stupid. They will not ask and you will never have the opportunity to answer the questions that really matter to your students if you are not willing to interact with them and become knowledgeable about their lives.

As a teacher in a given class, you need to ask yourself how you can build relationships with your students. With adults, a trip to a coffee shop or restaurant may be a good path. For many adults a shared meal in of one of your homes is the best path. Think in terms of a Christmas party or some similar reason. It almost sounds like a cliché to speak of men golfing together, hunting, or fishing while women shop, exercise, or take children to the park. If you are not a naturally outgoing person, you may need to make a real effort to look at how the culture you live in does relationship building. You are not trying to build a relationship for your sake but for the sake of your students. Your comfort is not the issue; that your students need to apply the Gospel in their lives is the issue. As a teacher you must build relationships to do your part in facilitating that growth. This is a vital step in teaching so ask God for His help and guidance and then work at building the needed relationships.

Children don't generally drink coffee and if they do it is usually not as social interaction with their teacher. Two generations ago it was common for grade school teachers to try to visit their students at home. This is much harder to accomplish in today's world. However, in very real ways you can never understand someone until you see where and to some extent how they live. An amazing amount of information can be gained about the home just by speaking with parents. It is remarkable what even brief interactions scattered over several weeks can tell you about a child's home life. Deserved praise of a student to his parent in his presence can also greatly enhance the willingness of the student to learn and apply teaching. But what if the parents are not involved with the church? Their absence alone tells you something. At the same time someone is bringing your student to the class and they are your adult source of information about the child.

If you work with children, you should never think of games during a class as just time fillers. They provide opportunities for you to have social interaction with your students and opportunities for your students to apply spiritual knowledge to life. Often games are the only opportunity for relationship building in a given class time. Games also provide an opportunity for students to apply or fail to apply the Gospel in life while you as the teacher can observe them. The obvious application of the Gospel is fair play and applied ethics, but just making sure that everyone is included shows that everyone has value. When you think in this way, you will deliberately plan any games for a learning purpose rather than just as fun time fillers. So when you are planning the lesson, ask yourself what kind of game lets you interact with the students and lets them live out the Gospel? The choices are plentiful, just think about why you are going to use a game and you will probably get it right.

Another way you can build relationships with children is to attend a school or sports events where they are involved. Ask the parents about this so you do not seem to be in any way improper. Have a class party a few times throughout the year and ask for parental help. Helping any child make a s'more will open doors. Take on a class project like helping with a food collection drive or litter removal. These kinds of activities will let you build relationships with the children, build relationships with the parents, and avoid any appearance of wrong kind of interest. Even if some parents are unsupportive, the presence of others will meet the need for transparency and those parents who do become involved will help you understand their children. If you are involved with some kind of group like the Assemblies of God's Royal Rangers, campouts with the proper safeguards can be pure gold in for building relationships and facilitating the application of head knowledge to life.

It is important to keep in mind why you need this relationship. Remember that Christianity is 'caught not taught'. You must seek relationship not for your sake or for its own sake but as a means of teaching. While in a classroom the focus may be on conveying facts the ultimate goal is faith in God and behavior that honors him. This cannot be taught with words and visual aids alone but must be modeled by the teacher and applied to the lives of the students. If there is no relationship, you cannot be a model. If there is no understanding of the students, there can be no accurate application. To teach others about the Lord you must know them and they must know you.

DISCUSSION QUESTIONS

1. Compare the nature of a true teacher to others who may fill the role.

2. What is the role of personal relationships to teaching?

3. What are some ways that you as a teacher have learned about your students?

4. How can you learn about students during class?

5. What purpose do social activities play in teaching?

4

Intentionality in
Teaching Techniques

NOTICE THAT TO THIS point teaching techniques have not been mentioned. Teaching techniques ought to vary greatly according to the students' background. Children of different ages require different techniques. Youth of different backgrounds require different methods. Adults of different backgrounds may require very different approaches. There are many books that discuss various teaching techniques in great detail. They will have listings and explanations for a large variety of teaching techniques. They will tell at what age you should use which technique. For adults, they often provide lists of techniques. As a teacher you need to educate yourself about appropriate techniques and approaches to different ages and groups.

You also need to develop wisdom to use the right approach to whatever group you are working with. Just because the technique is in a book does not make it right for your class. Sometimes the 'how to' books that focus on techniques for working in the church are pretty ridiculous. I own a book on witnessing written in the 1950s.[1] Its approach is very much like that of a vacuum cleaner

1. Lovett. Soul Winning is Easy.

salesman and even includes a picture of a vacuum cleaner sales-man as a positive example. It teaches how to maneuver people into admitting their need as sinners. It then explains how to persuade them to follow you in praying the sinner's prayer by the use of careful leading questions and even bodily positioning. For ex-ample, hold out a single finger about waist level while asking how many lies a person must have told to be a liar. It later instructs you to place your hand on the subject's shoulder and bow your own head. You are then told to wait patiently for the person to bow his head. I am not sure if this approach was successful in bringing people to Christ in the 1950s, but it seems unlikely to work in the present time.

Those who teach are teachers. As a teacher you need to think about what teaching techniques will work best with your class. Just because you are handed a book with lessons in it does not mean you are bound to its approach. The lesson book is the starting point for your teaching. As a teacher, and the teacher of a specific group you already know more about that group than any distant individual writing material for a generic class ever could. You may choose to try new ideas that are suggested. At the same time keep in mind that the ideas in the book are suggestions and are not im-posed upon you and your class. You are the one responsible before God for what you do in a given class.

In Paul's day, oratory was the big thing. To stand and speak with clever words and an impressive delivery was highly respected. Yet the Corinthians describe Paul saying, "in person he is unim-pressive and his speaking amounts to nothing." 2 Cor 10:10 NIV Paul himself admits that he was not an orator saying, "I may not be a trained speaker." 2 Cor. 11:6 NIV This is not your excuse to do a poor job teaching or to just stand and talk through the subject. Rather, it empowers you by releasing you from the need to have a degree in teaching to qualify as a teacher. It means that even if you do not excel at the most prestigious method in your time and place that you can still be very effective. You will have to use a variety of techniques. You do not have to be brilliant at them. You just have to use them the best you can. Then, like Paul, rely on the Holy Spirit to help you be effective.

Consider what approach the disciples would bring to the task of carrying out Christ's mandate: "teaching them to obey everything I have commanded you". Matt 28:20 NIV It is very unlikely that the apostles who "were unschooled and ordinary men" had even heard of Socrates or any other Greek teacher. Acts 4:13 NIV They were certainly not trained orators. Though they had not received any formal rabbinic training, they had been to synagogue all their lives. As a result what they did have was the experience of hearing the teachers of the Law and Jesus. To them teaching would be represented by these two examples. The teachers of the Law, even in light of the condemnation Jesus heaped upon them, likely provided the majority of instruction that the disciples received in their lifetime. This approach to teaching was the cultural norm and the disciples would on some level almost certainly imitate it. The methodology of teaching and the content taught are not the same thing. Jesus' example as a teacher was the focus of their lives for about three years. His use of stories, short sayings, object lessons, and questions would certainly influence their approach as well. The approach the disciples took to instructing others would likely be some mixture of these experiences.

In the same way you are the product of years in an educational system. Someone taught you about history, social studies, and government. Even if you did not pay much attention at the time you remember the approaches your teachers took. They lectured at times. They used a chalk board, or an electronic board, or an overhead projector, or PowerPoint. They showed you something while they were talking. They had handouts you could hold while you worked on the lesson. They brought in examples or at least showed you pictures of examples. Most likely they had you try out a role from time to time such as being a court or legislature. You probably had the equivalent of a show and tell time. In science they had you do experiments or showed them to you. Maybe they showed video of experiments. In your textbooks you read stories about relevant people or events. Maybe again that also happened by video. You memorized some facts from time to time. The teachers sometimes asked you or the class questions to help you think through the material. These represent a baseline of good and nearly universal teaching techniques in Western culture. The point is that just like the disciples, after 13 years of school you know more about teaching than you realize.

Since you already know a great deal about teaching you must make a thoughtful and prayerful application of this knowledge to the classes that you teach. Reading books on teaching techniques is not wrong; but, it will likely only remind you of things you already know on some level. You must decide before God what techniques will work best to teach a given lesson to your class. You must decide how to present the material so that the class is most likely to understand the material and apply it to their lives. This means that as a teacher you need to both pray and think a great deal not only about what passage means but how to teach the material. A poor match between your approach and a class will at best waste everyone's time and the opportunity for the students to learn more about the Lord. At worst, a really bad match between your approach and a class may leave people sufficiently put off that, they do not return to your class or perhaps any class. The limitation is that unless you receive some clear direct guidance from the Holy Spirit there will always be an element of simply making your best effort.

In approaching any class start with what kind of presentation is most likely to be effective with this age group? There are obvious differences between adults and children but there are also great differences between a five year old child and ten year old child. There are often surprisingly large differences between younger and older adults. As a real teacher you must think carefully and prayerfully about your class and seek to adopt the techniques best suited to your class.

An issue of similar effect is the background of your group of students. Rapidly presented charts and graphs are fine for those who handle such things regularly. For those who do not, the presentation must be slowed down to allow the material to be absorbed. Conversely, those who have cared for livestock and who have been up at all hours and out in all kinds of weather to take care of the animals will much more quickly understand the meaning and not just the words of Jacob who said:

> 38 "I have been with you for twenty years now. Your sheep and goats have not miscarried, nor have I eaten rams from your flocks. 39 I did not bring you animals torn by wild beasts; I bore the loss myself. And you demanded payment from me for whatever was stolen by day or night. 40 This was my situation: The heat consumed me in the daytime and the cold at night, and sleep fled from my eyes." Gen 31:38–40 NIV

As a teacher you need to ask yourself, are the approaches to presentation I am using appropriate for my students? In most classes dominated by older adults, asking them to act out an event in the Bible is not going to work. Almost anyone who has taught such a class understands this intuitively. However, for a group of children acting out a story may be an excellent approach. Those used to paper work and evaluations may readily accept a self-evaluation form, but a less paperwork oriented class may be put off. Your approach to teaching must take into account both the age and background of the people who will be in the class.

Therefore when deciding what teaching techniques to use, you need to think about the age, general cultural background and educational level of your class. Are they mostly white-collar office workers? Do they spend Monday through Saturday in an earthmover? Do they stock shelves for Walmart, repair cars, or teach school? Is your class filled with seniors or much younger adults? Are they all of the above mixed together? If you teach children, what is the experience of your age group in school? Three, six, and eleven year old children are very different. Their abilities and questions are different. Three year olds need to know that Jesus loves me. Eleven year olds are deciding what they believe about God and life. The age and life experience of your class will help you find a starting point for what teaching techniques are likely to work the best.

With any teaching technique you employ, you need to make a conscious effort to observe how students react to that particular approach. Do they sit up and listen? Will they willing fill out a survey or engage in role-play? Some seniors will act out roles in a moment and love it. Some younger people will refuse. You must experiment and watch how the class you are teaching responds to different approaches. You should pay attention to their responses and interaction in lecture. Are your students contributing by asking questions? Negatively, do they zone out and disengage from the class? Do one or two students do all the talking? Effective teachers will adjust their approach to the response of the class.

However, just because a class accepts a teaching approach and even responds does not mean that the approach is optimal. Children sometimes happily color pictures without the slightest thought of what the picture means. Many adults are sufficiently used to lecture that they accept it without any thinking or real learning. Some adult classes are nearly self-taught by discussion and happy with the situation. Acceptance of a given approach may only mean familiarity and safety. The question you must ask is, "does this approach promote learning and life change?"

A given technique may or may not be a good approach in a given class or with a particular passage or topic. It all depends on whether learning is occurring. Do the children understand the meaning of what they are coloring? Do they see any application of the story to their lives? In the case of a class dominated by discussion, all that may be happening is a portion of the class is demonstrating their current knowledge of the subject. It may even be nothing more than people who like to hear themselves talk and not even talking about the subject. As the teacher, you must find ways to evaluate what, if any, learning is occurring. If an approach is not resulting in learning in a given class, you need to use a different approach.

So how do you know if people are learning? I will touch the subject just briefly now as it will be the subject of a whole chapter later in the book. What education as a whole depends on is the written test. This is not, as a rule, well accepted by adults in

Sunday school or other small groups in churches. Children get written tests in school and generally have had enough during the week before they are in your class. However, you can ask questions. I even included multiple-choice questions at the end of a power point in a class of fifty blue-collar adults. They all answered together. This became a game for them and I could see they were getting the material. You can tie lessons together and pay attention to whether people are relating one to the other. Especially with children, you can play some kind of question game using the material. If you have a discussion, listen for references to earlier lessons. Really listen when students ask questions. Very often the questions asked will reveal whether learning is taking place. If learning does not seem to be taking place, ask God for wisdom and try different approaches.

Remember also from Jesus' example that the students' hearts must be open to receive the lesson. Jesus taught crowds who simply were not willing to receive the truth he was presenting to them. Likewise, Jesus' disciples also failed to grasp what He was teaching on numerous occasions. He repeatedly admonished them for the hardness of their hearts.[2] Jesus also said things that at times went beyond what the disciples seemed able to receive.[3] This was especially true of the statements He made about His death and resurrection. You will likely teach material that not everyone in the class will be able to receive at the time you teach it. Most classes are mixed to the extent that the people present have different background knowledge and different levels of maturity. Everyone will never get everything.

The conclusion is that you must match the techniques you use to the material and to your class. You must not just use whatever technique seems easiest or what the lesson says to do without considering how the approach will work with the people you are teaching. If you do you are likely to fail much of the time. Rather as a teacher you must adjust presentations to the experience and background of whomever you are teaching at a given time. This

2. Mark 9:10
3. Mark 8:17, Mark 6:52

means you must be flexible in how you teach. Most teachers are most comfortable with specific approaches. It is natural as people that they will favor the approaches they are most comfortable using. There may also be a laziness factor as some approaches to teaching require more preparation than others. Real teachers will care enough about their students to attempt to use whatever approach seems most likely to yield the best results. It is about your students' learning not your own comfort. As a teacher you must make the effort to use the best method for your specific group of students. Being a teacher requires that you be intentional about how you fulfill this ministry. Because you are responsible before God, you dare not simply slap something together or take what a lesson plan has without thinking about how it will or will not work with the material at hand and in your class.

DISCUSSION QUESTIONS

1. How can "how to" books on teaching techniques fall short?

2. How did the disciples learn to teach?

3. Why does designing a lesson for your particular class matter?

4. What are some issues you should consider when deciding how to teach a lesson to a class?

5. What are some ways the students in your class are different for others of about the same age?

5

Know the Material

Not many of you should presume to be teachers, my brothers, because you know that we who teach will be judged more strictly.

—Jas 3:1 NIV

TEACHERS ARE EXPECTED TO be knowledgeable of various points of doctrine, the interpretation of particular passages of Scripture, and background information. Students, especially children, often presume that the teacher knows the answer to everything about the Bible. If a teacher does not know things that a student thinks the teacher should know, it will hurt the teacher's credibility. If a teacher guesses or makes up an answer, his credibility may be destroyed when the student finds out the truth. If the student does not find out the truth, he might believe a lie the rest of his lives. This puts a heavy responsibility on teachers to know the material that they are teaching.

For some reading this book, the Bible has already been the focus of nearly a lifetime of study. For others who are new to teaching, parts of the Bible may still be a mystery. This is not a point of despair, but of challenge. If you do not know the Bible well, then you have to learn it. The best way to master the content of the Bible is simply to read it day by day. You should read a large enough section that you have the context to understand what it is about. You should ask God to help you understand and remember what the Bible says. Never lose sight of this truth: God's Word is God's Word. God knows what it means and He wants you to know as well. As you read, look carefully to see what God's Word actually says. Think about how the passage you read last week relates to what you are reading now. Write notes in the margin. Add your own cross-references.

This approach to reading means that you should probably avoid daily devotional guides. This is not an attack on your favorite guide but a simple matter of emphasis. The typical devotional guide has a few verses of Scripture and a few paragraphs of application. The authors of devotionals have many fine things to say about the Word, but what they write is not the Word. If you are going to learn God's Word you must read God's Word. Therefore, if you want a guide, try a chart that takes you through the Bible in a year.

This is not to say that you should not, that you must, avoid all outside help in reading the Bible. The rule, however, should always be to look for the answer in the place you are reading first, then in the rest of the Bible. A basic rule of Bible study is that Scripture interprets Scripture. Ask God for understanding. "Above all, you must understand that no prophecy of Scripture came about by the prophet's own interpretation. For prophecy never had its origin in the will of man, but men spoke from God as they were carried along by the Holy Spirit." 2 Peter 1:20–21 NIV If Scripture came by the Holy Spirit, then you should first ask the Holy Spirit to enable you to understand what is written. You will be amazed as you do this how much you begin to understand and remember.

Here is a good pattern for reading the Bible:

READ FOR CONTENT

- What does the text say?
- If something is unclear, read the passage in a different translation

READ FOR CONTEXT

- Look at the surrounding material
- To whom is this written?
- Who is mentioned?
- What is going on?

ASK WHAT DOES THIS PASSAGE MEAN?

- Try to put into words what the text says
- What are the big ideas?
- What principles does it teach?

    [There will be a whole chapter later devoted to principles]

ASK HOW DOES THIS APPLY TO MY LIFE?

- Is there something I should start doing?
- Is there something I should stop doing?
- Do I need to change my thinking in some way?
- Should I find special assurance or encouragement in this passage?

After you have tried to understand and are still struggling with a passage, then it is time to look at reference materials. The most common of these are commentaries, atlases, Bible dictionaries, Bible encyclopedias, and concordances. Commentaries are just what the name implies, comments by someone on the Bible. Bible atlases are usually a combination of maps and pictures of Bible objects and places. Bible encyclopedias have articles on specific places, things, people and ideas. Bible dictionaries are essentially the same thing as Bible encyclopedias, only smaller. A concordance is a listing of words in the Bible in alphabetic order and showing passages where they occur. A complete or exhaustive concordance has all the words in the Bible and all the places they occur. Cross reference works and topical works help you trace a specific subject through the whole of Scripture.

When something you have read just does not seem to make sense, a good reference to check is a commentary. Just remember, the Bible is God's Word, commentaries are just opinions from men and women. They vary greatly in quality and in approach. Some commentaries are mostly application of a given passage while others focus on explaining words and concepts. As a general rule, commentaries written by individuals on a single book in the Bible are better than commentaries written by one person on the whole Bible. Sets of commentaries of both kinds are available. Before you spend money for any commentary, try looking up two or three passages you are familiar with and see what is said. Think about whether the content helps you understand the passage. Always be aware that the author, like everyone else, has a theological perspective which will affect how a passage is explained.

Often a good Bible atlas will help you in understanding a passage by showing locations and the distances involved in travel. A good atlas will also show the terrain. Plaines, mountains, hills, valleys, and badlands each allow and prohibit certain activities. The early Israelites usually fought on foot, often against enemies who used horse-drawn chariots. As a result, they often attacked from the hills against chariot-borne enemies. David hid from Saul in very rough terrain in the south of the country. A good atlas should help you see such things so you can better understand what is happening and why. Pay attention to the scale of the map. Israel is a small country. If you are accustomed to the scales used in American highway maps you can be easily confused about the scale of distances as shown in atlases. It is only about 65 miles from the Sea of Galilee to the Dead Sea and only about 28 miles from the Sea of Galilee to the Mediterranean Sea.

Most atlases also have pictures. These vary greatly in quality and often show ruins or broken artifacts with little context. Some will include modern artists' interpretations of how something appeared in ancient times. These, like commentaries, are interpretations and because of their visual nature can deeply affect your understanding. If they depict specific objects found in Scripture at least be sure the picture matches the Bible's description. In one widely used study Bible there is a drawing of the basins used for water in Solomon's temple. The wheels as shown are very small and do not match the Bible's description. They would work poorly in handling these very heavy carts. Another picture in a commentary shows the pillars on the porch of Solomon's Temple with smoke coming from them. This has no basis in Scripture. In the artist's comments he explains that he had read of a pagan temple built this way and simply decided on his own that Solomon's Temple must have been the same. This is not to down-play the value of modern representations but it is a warning to look at them with a critical eye.

A Bible dictionary or encyclopedia is most useful when you are looking up something specific like a place, object, person or idea. They also include introductions to the books of the Bible and generally have outlines for them. The articles are written by many different scholars and then edited to fit into the overall book. A typical use for such a book would be looking up the town of Bethlehem or King Ahab. Looking up grace would give you the main passages where it is mentioned and a summary of the idea. A good test for dictionaries would be to look up the meaning of the mandrakes found by Reuben in Gen 30:14. Again, remember that the articles are written by people with their own perspectives about the Bible. They are not inspired; they are simply human beings trying to help you understand. In selecting a Bible dictionary or encyclopedia, look up several names and subjects. Ask yourself if the information helps you understand. The answer will help you pick resources that are useful to you.

Many of these resources are available in electronic form and combined into integrated computer programs. The cost of these varies, but most start at well over a hundred dollars and go up to over a thousand dollars. This can provide great benefits but there are also real limitations. One of the greatest benefits of a computer program is that it can usually perform very specific concordance searches. You can generally limit where in the Bible you want to look such as the New Testament or even individual books. Computers allow you to search for passages that include two or more words that you want to find together such as grace and peace. They will also allow you to search for a phrase. In addition, computer searches display more of the text than paper concordances and allow you to move instantly to the passage or passages you have found. Computer programs also let you cross-reference any dictionaries or commentaries that are included and some will show you relevant maps as well. They can speed up your study by providing multiple kinds of information very quickly. They can be very useful.

The great weakness of such programs is that they often come bundled with old, out of copyright material and emphasize quantity over quality. Some programs will let you buy and add up-to-date material but the cost is often nearly as great as paper copies. Moreover, you generally must update the program when you update your computer's operating system. Often these updates are quite expensive and may even equal the original purchase price. Another drawback is that if a publisher goes out of business or drops the program you may be only one operating system update from losing everything. Remember Windows 95? As a result, if you like the idea of this kind of integrated study you may be best off buying only a basic program for your computer and expensive references in paper. How many today even remember Microsoft Works, Office Star, or WordPerfect? Fifty-year-old books still work.

Why am I ignoring the internet? It is easy, it is free, and google knows everything. More accurately, google indexes everything. The internet has some excellent material available. The problem is that the internet is also full of garbage. This garbage is probably the biggest problem on the web for most teachers rather than flagrant heresy. Because of this garbage, you must exercise careful judgment concerning anything you find online. Anyone,, whether they know anything or not, can put up a website. Google will then find it and list it for you to use. Consequently, you must not take information from just any source without thinking about where the website's author got the information or whether they just made it up. Otherwise good people who find apparently amazing information love to spread what they have learned. The problem is that they spread the information whether it is true or not. Many websites contain information that is imaginary because the truth is simply unknown. Specifically, the internet contains much supposed cultural background material that is completely false. If you use information that is just made up or a lie, you then become responsible before God for imposing that lie on your class. One great reason you need to learn solid background material is so that you can identity questionable material.

Cleverly packaged heresy is another danger found on the internet. Remember, anyone can put up a website. You will also find the Mormons, Jehovah's Witnesses, and a wide selection of cults and heretics posting on the internet. While some of these are clearly labeled and upfront about their viewpoints and sources, many others are not. When using the internet, you need to be sufficiently knowledgeable about the truth to spot the problems. Websites can be like mouse poison. If you read the ingredients on a box of mouse poison you will find that it is ninety-nine percent good food and less than one percent poison. The problem is that the less than one percent that is poison can kill you. When you use websites without thinking critically about what they may be promoting you risk ingesting the one percent and also passing it on to your class.

So what can you find on the web that is useful and reasonably safe to use? First and foremost, the web excels in providing you with original material from classic sources such as Josephus, the ante-Nicaean church fathers, John Calvin, John Wesley, and many others. You can read the same information that the people writing most of study material use. I recently quoted a Roman humorist named Juvenal making fun of Jews to show that the culture had a general knowledge of Judaism. After all the joke would not have been funny if it had to be explained. I got the information by remembering that I had seen something about it, then I used google to locate the writings of Juvenal online and finally I used a document search to find the joke. It took only a few minutes total. Having seen for myself, I do not have to wonder if someone just made the story up. This allowed me to present the information to my class with confidence in its accuracy. The real surprise to me was that the joke Juvenal told required that the general culture have a far more detailed knowledge of Judaism that I would have guessed.

The internet will also give you access to numerous older commentaries. The key point to understand is that these commentaries are all at least a hundred years old because to be posted in this way means that they are out of copyright. That does not mean these resources cannot be useful. I have used many of them on different occasions. Two sites that have been reliable in the past and give you good access to these older commentaries are Biblehub.com and Studylight.org/commentaries. These sites also act as super concordances allowing you to search phrases and quickly check multiple translations. In short, they are very like the less expensive programs you could purchase and load on your home computer. Another somewhat more comprehensive site is Biblestudytools. com which includes Bible dictionaries and atlases. However, all the books I have found on these sites are old enough to be out of copyright. A site devoted to maps is Bibleatlas.org which is up-to-date and has outstanding maps that are free to use. There are many other websites, but always remember, internet sites and their content tend to appear and disappear regularly. The ones I just mentioned may be gone by the time you get this book. Also remember that no matter where you find them, commentaries are simply men's comments on the Bible. Some are better than others and none are infallible.

If you want anything worthwhile written since WW1, most of the time you are going to have to pay for it. If you want the resource in an electronic form, many can be purchased through the Bible programs mentioned earlier or book sellers such as Christianbook.com or Amazon.com. Paper copies are available for nearly everything and used copies are cheaper. Some exceptions to the requirement to pay for recent materials are some academic journals and college syllabi which are posted online as a service. These are usually very narrowly focused and it can be hard to find information about a specific passage. They have the advantage that the cultural background information they contain has been cross checked by others and is usually reliable.

A good way to picture these resources is as a toolbox. You have tools to help you with various tasks. Pliers let you grip much tighter than you can with your fingers alone. In the same way, a Bible dictionary gives you an expanded vocabulary greater than you have now. Just as you have many different kinds of tools in a toolbox you will need several different kinds of resources to help you with deeper Bible study. No one resource will help you with every task. Over time you will also acquire more than one of each type of resource. After all, how many screwdrivers do you typically have? How many different kinds of pliers do you own? In the same way, Bible study resources, even in the same general type have strengths, weaknesses, and specialties which you will discover over time. Just as in any other vocation, as a teacher you are going to need a tool box. Ask God to help you to invest wisely in the tools you buy.

DISCUSSION QUESTIONS

1. What is the best approach for you personally in reading the Bible?

2. What is a Bible commentary?

3. How can a commentary be useful? An atlas? A Bible Dictionary?

4. What are some values of electronic resources?

5. What are some weakness and dangers of electronic resources?

6

There Are Some Things
You Just Need to Know!

ALONG WITH READING AND studying, there are some things you
should just KNOW. For example, if you do not already know them,
you need to learn the books of the Bible in order. Fumbling around
trying to find a reference while your class looks on is just embar-
rassing. Adults may be somewhat forgiving; children can be brutal
in their opinions. The Bible is the WORD of GOD. It is the focus of
your effort and calling as a teacher. When you do not know where
the books in Bible are located, it tells your students that they certainly do not need to know. For both your own and your students'
sake you need to know where the books of the Bible are located so
that you can easily find references in it.

A second thing you should just know is the 10 Commandments
and where to find them in the Bible. Many churches have
them posted somewhere. Christians love to have them displayed
in public places. You probably already know most of them but you
need to know all of them and in order. Imagine some visitor or a
child challenging you, "I'll bet you don't even know the 10 Commandments!" If you know them you have the upper hand in that
lesson and many more to come. If you don't, it will not be a happy

day. You do not even have to know all the details of each commandment just the equivalent of the title is usually enough

Everyone who is a believer should have some verses of the Bible memorized. As a teacher, you especially need a plan to memorize some key passages. The first great benefit of knowing Scripture by memory allows you to meditate on the Bible as God instructed us to do. As you ponder a passage over time, it will change your thinking. The Holy Spirit will give you understanding that rarely comes in any other way. You will see applications to your own life and ultimately to your teaching. The second great benefit comes while you are teaching. When you have verses memorized, the Holy Spirit can bring these verses to your mind while you are teaching. Sometimes this is in answer to a question; sometimes, it just helps you explain what you had already planned to say. It is both an amazing and humbling experience to have the Spirit use you in this way. However, it only happens when you know Scripture verses by heart.

Many people have drawn up lists of Scriptures that that they believe you should memorize. Most of these really do have pretty good balance to them and cover critical doctrinal points. They can be a good starting point for deciding what to memorize. Another approach is to pick out verses and sections that stand out to you as you read. This is not as systematic an approach but has the advantage of personal meaning. It can be far easier to learn a passage that means something to you than a seemingly random assortment of verses chosen by an expert. The way you select verses to memorize is not as important as getting verses memorized.

There are a variety of strategies people have used for the process of memorizing Bible verses. Some people have had great success using index cards with the passage on one side and the reference on the other. They go through their stack alternating sides daily. They add new cards about once a week. Other people post a verse of the week where they will see it over and over repeating it each time it is seen. The tech savvy may use recorded verses in their earphones or app on their favorite electronic device. The method used in memorizing Scripture is less important than that you are memorizing Scripture. Whatever approach you use, be sure to review the verses you have learned periodically so that your effort is not lost.

Here are some well tested ideas on memorizing Scripture

HELPS FOR HOW TO START
MEMORIZING SCRIPTURE

- Pick a verse that speaks to you.
- Check recommended lists for verses to memorize.
- Say the reference before and after the verse.
- Read the verse aloud many times.
- Record several of your verses and use looping digital play back
- Break the verse into natural phrases.
- Emphasize key words when quoting the verse.
- Write out the verse on a card with the reference on the other side.
- Go through the cards daily reversing front and back.
- Display your verses where you will see them often and quote them when you do.
- Always memorize the verse word–perfect.
- Some verses have been set to music. This is limited but can really help.
- Get a partner for accountability

In order to really read with understanding, you will need to know in at least general terms who wrote the most referenced books and when. This goes hand in glove with knowing a general timeline of the Old and New Testaments. This is not usually something you just memorize but as you read through the Bible you will be learning much of the timeline. This is especially true of the Old

Testament. It will help you greatly if you read a short introduction to each book of the Bible as you start reading it. These should give you authorship and general historical context. Nearly every study Bible has these introductions. Bible dictionaries or books with titles like *Introduction to the Old [or New] Testament* have longer ones. If you will just faithfully read your Bible and include these as you go you will have this information quickly enough.

In most teaching situations in the church, there is a teacher's guide or something similar to follow. These are designed to be starting points for lesson preparation. To be effective as a teacher, you have to adapt the material to the students you actually have in the class. Most books at this point have a discussion about various techniques for how to teach the material. This begs the questions of what material should be taught. Your teacher's guide probably gives you a starting passage and commentary on the passage. Usually, there are also some applications and recommended techniques for presentation. As a teacher, you need to really understand the passage yourself. This means reading and knowing the immediate context of the passage but also understanding the place of the passage in the light of the whole Bible. This kind of knowledge allows you to explain the passage to your students, not just parrot what someone has said in a generic way. It also helps you make accurate applications of the passage for your students. When they ask a question, you can give a reasoned answer rather than an off the cuff response you may regret later. It makes it possible for you to teach your students rather than just regurgitate what someone who never met your class wrote down several years ago for a study guide. The knowledge to do this is gained by study of God's Word over time.

Many of you are thinking this sounds good but 'I am teaching a class right now.' It will take years to learn the Bible the way this guy is talking about. Actually, it takes a lifetime and there is always more to learn. More than one teacher has had to spend time mastering material week by week ahead of his class. However, if class preparation is all the study you do, you will never really learn God's Word and you will never really be very good as a teacher.

Frankly, you ought to do both your preparation for class and your own study that has nothing at all to do what any class you are teaching. This is the same approach pastors are taught during their training. You may not be a pastor but you handle God's Word just the same and the same approach applies.

The simple truth is this: to teach God's Word you must know God's Word. This takes time and effort. Knowing God's Word is part of the calling of a teacher. The effort required to know God's Word is a part of the cost of the ministry of teaching. However, this knowledge is also a blessing to a teacher in his own life. God's Word will guide you in difficulties, correct you in sin, and comfort you in in sorrow. Nothing else on this earth will do in your life what a deep knowledge of the Word of God will do for you.

When you struggle to understand and apply the Word in your own life and in your teaching, you can claim a special promise Jesus gave to His disciples:

> "All this I have spoken while still with you. 26 But the Counselor, the Holy Spirit, whom the Father will send in my name, will teach you all things and will remind you of everything I have said to you. John 14:25–26 NIV

God wants you to do a good job as a teacher. He has promised to help your memory and your understanding. Just keep in mind that the Holy Spirit can only bring back to your memory that which you have in your memory and only give you understanding of what you have studied. If you know what is in the Bible, the Holy Spirit can remind you of what it says and what it means. On the occasions that happens while you are teaching this is a humbling and awesome experience.

DISCUSSION QUESTIONS

1. What is the value in just knowing some basic information from the Bible?

2. What are some things you think a teacher should just know?

3. Which suggestion for memorizing Scripture do you think would help you the most?

4. While you were teaching, have you had the Holy Spirit bring to your mind verses you have memorized?

5. How does a strong knowledge of the Bible allow you to adapt lessons to your class?

7

Teach Principles

Then God said, "Take your son, your only son, Isaac, whom you love, and go to the region of Moriah. Sacrifice him there as a burnt offering on one of the mountains I will tell you about."

—Gen 22:2 NIV

We seem to understand intuitively that this instruction is only for Abraham and is not an instruction we are all to follow. Most, with a little more experience reading Scripture, will explain quickly that this story shows God testing Abraham to see who has first place in Abraham's life. Then we could look for the underlying idea behind the test. We could state the idea as: God demands absolute first place in our lives above everything else. These underlying ideas are called principles. A principle is an idea that underlies a given passage of Scripture. Using principles allows us to apply scripture to circumstances across a broad width of cultural situations. The principle that God demands absolute first place in our lives above everything else can be applied to not just Isaac but to anything! God must come before money, fame, pleasure, family, or even our physical lives.

Another example of a passage where the principle can easily be seen is Eph 5:18. "Do not get drunk on wine, which leads to debauchery". Eph 5:18 NIV This passage very clearly forbids becoming drunk on wine. However, there is still also a principle underlying this command. We can state this as: do not use substances to impair your judgment. Finding this principle lets us apply Eph 5:18 not just to wine but also to the other obvious alcohols like beer and hard liqueur. However, this principle is much broader. It also forbids the use of LSD, THC, and many other drugs that would have been unknown to Paul but which have the same effect as wine in impairing judgment. Using principles lets us apply the Bible to new situations that did not exist when it was written.

Finding principles and applying them to a person's current situation is not some modern invention. It is definitely not a way to get around Scripture. It is found within Scripture and is used by both Jesus and Paul. When Paul is admonishing the Corinthians that ministers deserve to be paid, he quotes Deut 25:4, "Do not muzzle an ox while it is treading out the grain." At first, this seems very far from the issue Paul is addressing. Paul then says in 1Cor 9:10, "when the plowman plows and the thresher threshes, they ought to do so in the hope of sharing in the harvest." The idea is that those who do the work should profit from the work. This applies right down to the animal pulling a threshing sledge. Paul then gives his application in 1Cor 9:14, "In the same way, the Lord has commanded that those who preach the gospel should receive their living from the gospel."

This way of dealing with Scripture is called principle/application. It means you figure out what idea Scripture is teaching, that is the principle, and then apply it to your situation. Sometimes this is very easy when the Scripture passage itself is in the form of a principle. "You shall not murder." Exod. 20:13 NIV Is in the form of a principle as it is stated. It requires only application. There are plenty of other principles stated directly in Scripture. However, whether you have to look carefully to see the underlying principle or if it is immediately apparent, all principles require application on some level. Much of the work of teaching is extracting these principles and explaining their application.

An important way to check to see if what you think is the underlying idea or principle in a passage is to ask if the same principle is taught elsewhere in Scripture. In the example of Abraham and Isaac our principle was that God demands first place in our lives above everything. This can clearly be found in several places including "Love the Lord your God with all your heart and with all your soul and with all your strength." Deut 6:5 NIV and "37 Jesus replied: "'Love the Lord your God with all your heart and with all your soul and with all your mind.' 38 This is the first and greatest commandment." Matt 22:37-38 NIV When we find agreement like this, we can have confidence that what we have stated as a principle accurately reflects what the Scripture passage is teaching. You should also ask if any statement in Scripture contradicts what you think is a principle. Clearly, Scripture does not contradict Scripture. If you can find a passage that contradicts what you think is a principle, you do not have a Scriptural principle.

Jesus uses the principle/application approach when the Pharisees challenge him over His disciples working on the Sabbath by plucking heads of wheat so that they could eat. Matt 12:1-12 records the exchange between Jesus and the Pharisees. In this case, Jesus provides three separate Scriptural bases for the principle that He states, "it is lawful to do good on the Sabbath." Matt 12:12 NIV Jesus begins by mentioning the story of David eating the Showbread from the Tabernacle when he was in need. David is in a difficult situation and the ceremonial law is superseded by the practical need. Nowhere is either David or the priest who gave him the bread condemned for the action. Jesus then points out that the priests work in the Temple on every Sabbath. In their work priests butcher numerous animals. This is functionally no different from what many people do on the other six days. God Himself commanded this labor and no one thinks that the priests preforming this service are sinning. Finally Jesus quotes Hos 6:6 "I desire mercy, not sacrifice" to show God's priority of human need over ceremony. The application is that the disciples' behavior of picking and eating nearly ripe grain on the Sabbath is not sinful.

Both Jesus and Paul also illustrate the principles that they draw from Scripture. Jesus does this when the Pharisees continue to attack Him by shifting their focus from obtaining food to healing on the Sabbath. Jesus illustrates the principle that it *is* lawful to do good on the Sabbath by pointing out that if they had a sheep that fell into a well on the Sabbath that they would immediately lift it out. He then heals a man with a withered hand and points out that men are more valuable than sheep. Together these are both an illustration and an application of the principle.

Remember Paul's principle that those who do the work should profit from the work. In his construction of the argument to the Corinthians Paul actually precedes the statement of this principle with three of his illustrations. He asks, "Who serves as a soldier at his own expense? Who plants a vineyard and does not eat of its grapes? Who tends a flock and does not drink of the milk?" 1 Cor 9:7 NIV After Paul states this principle, his references to plowmen and threshers serve as additional illustrations. The obvious answer is anyone working in any of these ways is paid and usually the pay derives from the work he is doing. The application that Paul wants the Corinthians to make of this is paying their ministers.

The pattern for identifying a principle is to look at a Scripture passage and ask what idea the passage is teaching. Sometimes this is very easy as with the Ten Commandments. Sometimes in narrative passages there may be several principles taught. However, especially with narrative passages, you need to be careful that you are taking the ideas out of the passage and not adding your own ideas into the passage. Consider the story of David and Goliath. If you are trying to assign meaning to each of the stones David carried, you are probably adding your ideas into the passage. If you are looking at the big picture of what is going on and say something like, God is with us when we face big problems, you are probably finding principles. A good indication of whether you are finding the principle or assigning your own meaning is if you can think of other places in Scripture where the same principle is taught.

When the principle is not obvious we must ask why God included this in His Word to us. For example God commands in the Law, "When you build a new house, make a parapet around your roof so that you may not bring the guilt of bloodshed on your house if someone falls from the roof." Deut 22:8 NIV The command comes from the common practice in Biblical times of building houses with flat roofs that serve as patios for the residents. You can see this in the story of the two spies hidden by Rahab on her roof under bundles of flax. Since it is uncommon for us to build a flat roof where we intend to walk or work, this passage seems to have little to do with our lives. However, ask yourself what is the idea behind this command. The key is the reason given in the second half of the verse, "so that you may not bring the guilt of bloodshed on your house if someone falls from the roof". The concern is that someone could fall and that you should install a railing to keep everyone safe. A general principle that could be drawn from this is, if you build something that could endanger others, build in safety devices. Applications might include placing a railing on stairs or balconies, placing a guard on a power saw, or placing child protective covers on outlets. An illustration could be almost any situation where a safety device was clearly needed but not installed and someone was hurt.

This is a good place to stop and ask if the principle, *if you build something that could endanger others, build in safety devices*, is taught elsewhere in Scripture. Remember, if something is actually a principle from the Word it will be taught in more than one place. In this case, there are at least two passages with ideas that are close parallels to this principle: Exod 21:28-29 distinguishes between someone killed by a bull and someone killed by a bull that is known to be dangerous. In the first case only the bull is killed. This is a serious loss to the owner but nothing more is done. In contrast, God holds the owner of a bull that is known to be dangerous accountable if he has not penned it up and it hurts others–in this case, life for life. The same principle is behind this passage as the principle behind the command that a railing must be put around a roof. If you know that something is dangerous you must take steps to protect others. Again, Exod 22:6 says if you start a fire but fail to control it you are responsible for any damage that the fire causes. Thus, the principle behind this passage is the same. Although fire is useful and we will use fire, it is inherently dangerous. As a result when we start a fire we are responsible to protect others from our actions. We can conclude from these supporting examples that our principle is taught in several places in Scripture. It is truly a principle from God's Word that, if you build something that could endanger others, you must build in safety devices.

Whatever God is saying to us in Scripture will have principles behind it that God wants us to understand. God knew when he dealt with Abraham that we would be reading about it four thousand years later. God knew that people scattered around the world and throughout the rest of history would read the Law given to Moses, the history of Israel, the words of the prophets, and the poetry of the Psalms. God knew that His Church would speak in many very different languages and live in many radically different cultures than ancient Israel. God therefore gave us Scripture structured in such a way that people living at any time and living in any culture could make use of His Word. The means He used is that of placing principles behind the Bible that can be applied in any time and any culture.

Whatever passage of Scripture you are teaching from, you should look for the principles God is teaching in that passage. Often, if you are using a lesson book, it will have a central truth or something similar. This central truth is usually a principle drawn from the passage. As the teacher you may want to use this principle or you may look for a different one from the passage that fits your class better. Only remember the rule is that any principle that you correctly derive from a passage will also be taught elsewhere in the Bible and cannot be contradicted anywhere in the Bible.

Searching out principles and making correct applications of them is a heavy responsibility that requires a good knowledge of Scripture and its cultural and historical background. This is why you need to know the material in Scripture and the cultural and historical background of Scripture. As a teacher you interpret

Scripture to your students–that is you explain what it means. Essentially, you find and explain principles. You are responsible to make correct applications of those principles to their lives. Finally, you must then illustrate the principle or principles you are teaching so that the students understand the meaning for their lives.

The good news is that as a teacher God has gifted you to do this. The Scripture that you are charged to teach others is inspired by the Holy Spirit. The same Holy Spirit who inspired the Scripture dwells inside of you and enables you to understand Scripture. The same Holy Spirit helps you to see the principles of the Bible and their application to your life and the lives of your students. The Spirit will help you to find the right illustrations to make these principles clear to your students. God is with you to help you do this and do it well for His glory.

DISCUSSION QUESTIONS

1. What is a Bible principle? Give an example.

2. How does the principle you focus on in a passage affect your lesson preparation?

3. How does using principles make the Bible relevant throughout history and across cultures?

4. How is principle different from application?

5. What is an example of a principle you have taught recently?

8

Teaching That Truly Educates Your Students

A REAL TEACHER CARES about whether learning is taking place. After all, this is the purpose of teaching. Remember, in the church, teaching means far more than imparting the skill of doing long division or grasping and applying historical trends to current events. Effective teaching in the church means that students know the content of the Word of God, understand what the Word of God means, and can apply the Word of God in a way that they can live it out in their lives. These are the three objectives you are seeking to achieve in every lesson. These objectives or goals build on one another, as you must know the facts before you can understand them and understanding precedes proper application.

As a teacher, your responsibility is to present the information in the way best suited to the learning style of the students in a given class. This starts with your prayers and best effort. However, you ultimately need to have some means of knowing if the students are learning the material that you are presenting. Do they grasp the information? Do they understand the information? Can they apply the information in their lives? The answers to these questions tell you whether your current teaching methods are working. If your current teaching methods are working, you can keep using them. If the current teaching methods are not working, you can make adjustments.

So how do you know if your students are learning what you are teaching? The most immediate and often the best feedback comes from watching their faces. You can quickly tell if students are bored or interested. Look at the posture of the students. Are they sitting forward? If you have adults watch to see if they are taking notes, looking something up, or leaned back with their arms crossed. Children who are bored will quickly reveal their attitude—usually in unpleasant ways. Children who are engaged, show it with far fewer inhibitions than adults do. If you just watch the class while you are teaching you can usually tell whether the approach you are using is working.

This is, however, only the first step. Sometimes a class may be engaged but is either not getting the material or is failing to understand the material. To know if learning is really taking place you must get more feedback than is possible from facial expressions and body language alone. You really cannot know if your teaching is effective without additional feedback. There are a variety of ways to gain this feedback; some of which work better with adults and some work better with children. To be effective in teaching, you will have to work out which ways of gaining feedback work best with those you are teaching.

In both adults and children, the first approach is simply to ask questions. The key is asking the right questions the right way. Generally, any question that can be answered with either a yes or a no is not very helpful in gaining feedback. The opposite extreme of a completely open ended question such as, "Does anyone wish to add anything?" has its own troubles. Everyone has heard Bro. X go on and on about something he heard on the news this week. Sometimes what Bro. X says is even a little bit related to the class. Good questions avoid both extremes and help you see if learning is taking place.

Good questions gain feedback first on whether the students have grasped the content of God's Word being presented in a lesson. That is, did they get the content you were teaching? Questions to determine if student have gained the information you are teaching are generally of the who, what, and where variety. Who did what to whom? What happened? Where did it happen? You need to know if the students have understood the basic facts or content of the lesson. There can be no understanding or application without first knowing the content. Feedback showing success in the area of content lets you move on to understanding and application.

If students did not get the information, you need an instant review. Sometimes just saying the same thing again in different words is enough. Often some of the class has received the information even if not everyone has. The answers given by those who know can help inform those who do not. Nevertheless, try to get responses from a variety of students and not just the few who always have the answer. If you do not make an effort to involve everyone, those not inclined to provide instant answers might mentally withdraw. Regaining their attention can be difficult and is sometimes impossible. You pretty much have to keep reviewing until students get the content since you cannot understand either meaning or application without the facts.

With most adult classes, your choices for additional feedback are limited. Often you can use some kind of quiz if it is informal and no one thinks he or she will stand out as being wrong. I have successfully used both fill in the blank and multiple-choice quizzes by putting them in PowerPoint slides and having everyone answer at once. Those who know the answers have their knowledge reinforced and those who do not know hear the material presented again. In an academically astute class, you may be able to use oral quizzes directed to individuals and maybe even written quizzes on some occasions.

Sometimes quizzes can be a teaching tool in and of themselves. I personally have a "Christmas Quiz" that is exceptionally difficult. I make a game of having students fill it in and see who can do the best. No one does well. I then go over the quiz in class making sure everyone has the answers. When the exercise is over, I have taught the content. This has worked well for me; and, students get the content.

With children, there are a greater variety of other approaches for reviewing and making certain that the students have learned the content. Most involve a game of some kind where winning involves knowing the facts of the content. There are scores of possibilities but this book is not focused on technique. However, using games in a class to simultaneously teach and review content with children is a time tested and effective method. Hand in hand with using games is the use of small prizes for success in the game or just paying attention and knowing. Memory verses are a special kind of content knowledge and giving prizes for learning assigned verses can be very effective.

Using hands-on activities is the norm with smaller children. Used properly they can be very useful in helping make certain the children have received the content. However, it is critical to tie the activity to the information. When coloring a picture of David and his sling or making a toy sling to throw nerf balls you can ask, who is involved and what is happening. Perhaps most importantly you can ask what something means. This can both reinforce content and help you make certain that the child has received the content. If you use activities and do not tie them to the Biblical content, you are wasting the very limited time available to change children's lives.

The second part of the learning is understanding the information. Knowing a 'fact' and understanding something of its meaning is not the same thing. There is the story of a man whose young son asked, "Where babies come from?" The man takes a deep breath and then provides a clear description of sex. The son is somewhat incredulous and looking at his infant sister says, "So you and mom did that twice?" The point is that mere factual knowledge is unequal to understanding. It is not enough simply to know the facts; you must also have some understanding of what the facts mean.

A starting point in looking for understanding might be to ask a student to restate the idea in his or her own words. Success at least shows general comprehension. Another related approach is to ask if students can summarize the information. These questions can establish that general understanding is in place. These kinds of questions are likely to be most successful with children or teens. They can quickly let you establish what level of understanding is present. You can then move forward to expanding understanding and ultimately application of God's Word in their lives.

Asking the right open-ended questions (questions that have no immediate right answer) can also help you look for understanding. Consider a lesson that was about how David eluded Saul in the wilderness. Do not ask, "Who chased David in the wilderness?" This requires only the factual answer, Saul. Instead, you should ask, "What are some ways that David handled conflict with Saul?" Answers to this kind of question require information but also understanding of what is happening. Answers might include David first remained steady with Saul hoping that Saul would change. David also sought the intercession of others like Jonathan before running away. You could see if students really understood David's attitude by asking about his rebuke of his subordinates who wanted him to kill Saul in the cave and elsewhere.

Another way of looking for expanded understanding is asking if someone can give you an illustration of the idea in the lesson. This shows if they can take the information and apply it in a different context. You are looking to see if the analogy that the student builds accurately reflects the meaning of the lesson. A slightly different tactic is to ask the class how they would explain the information to someone who had not heard the lesson. Both approaches require understanding of the information for the illustration to fit and the explanation to be accurate. With younger students, these questions might be asked directly. When working with adults these questions usually are worked into more general class discussion.

When understanding seems slow in coming, you as the teacher may need to use an illustration to move the discussion forward. Good lesson planning means that you should have something ready if it is needed. Sometimes you can create an illustration on the spot. Here is a place the Holy Spirit can help you by illuminating your mind with the right explanation. When the Spirit moves in this way, you will sometimes amaze your students. You will also be amazed since you know that you did not plan what you just said and generally because you know you are not that smart.

Once you are reasonably sure the students understand the material, it is vital that they see how to apply the knowledge to their lives. We often say that it means people must not just have knowledge in their heads and then let it drop the eighteen inches to their hearts. Bear in mind that we are admonished, "Knowledge puffs up, but love builds up".1 Cor 8:1–2 NIV Therefore, our ultimate goal in any lesson must be behavioral use of what is taught and not merely knowledge. Knowledge about God that is not acted upon is worse than useless. The goal is knowledge of God that is lived out in daily life. This life application of information must be the goal of all Christian teaching.

Since most application will take place after students leave the class, deciding if students can apply the lesson in their lives is the most difficult goal to measure. We are trying to know future behavior. Clearly, this is impossible with certainty. We can seek to know, if they know, how to be obedient to this portion of God's Word. Discussion is always a good starting point. Questions such as "What would or should you do if . . . ?" come at the objective directly. Asking for any response that involves the students applying the material will at least move your students in the right direction.

If the students are willing, this is where role-playing can have great effect. Actually practicing the desired behavior is a good way to learn a behavior. Not every class is willing to engage in role-play and not every lesson lends itself to the technique but when it fits, it is a good choice. It will literally let you watch and see if the students can apply the material. If you do plan on using role-playing, think carefully about the scenario you ask people to play through. If it is too obvious, you may gain nothing, if it is to complex the students will get lost. You need to use wisdom to get it right.

One of the best ways to find out if the students applied the part of God's Word you taught in one lesson is to inquire about it in the next class session. One way to do this with children is the use of feedback sheets from parents. You are in essence giving a homework assignment. Whether or not you can do this effectively depends greatly upon the families of the children you are dealing with. Some curriculum includes take home sheets for every lesson. If you use take home sheets as an evaluation tool, you must find a way to get them either back or at least talk about them in the next class. With adults you can simply ask the students at the beginning of the next class about how they we able to follow through on the lesson from the previous week. This can be done positively in the form of testimonies. Asking these kinds of questions can be awkward—especially if no one is willing to speak up. However, it directly addresses whether or not students applied the lesson in their lives. You will need to seek God for wisdom; but, at least try this approach.

Although it only fits a lesson occasionally, direct application of the material can be done on some lessons. When it does fit, it will show you as the teacher if you succeeded in the application goal right before your eyes. Examples might include praying for the sick present or for those who are absent. Have people pray about witnessing activities. A class on kindness or good works might end with a plan of how to carry out such an act. A lesson on missions can end in prayer and an offering. This can be done with both adults and children.

We are charged as teachers with imparting knowledge to our students. This includes knowing information, understanding information and applying information. However, information and understanding without application is worse than ignorance!

> 47"That servant who knows his master's will and does not get ready or does not do what his master wants will be beaten with many blows. 48 But the one who does not know and does things deserving punishment will be beaten with few blows. Luke 12:47–48 NIV

As teachers we cannot insure that our students will obey the message of God's Word. However, we must make every effort to see that students know how to apply a given lesson. Then we must urge them to be obedient to that lesson in their lives.

DISCUSSION QUESTIONS

1. What role does feedback play in discovering if learning is happening?

2. How have you found out that students either understood or did not understand something you taught?

3. Give an example of a good question to ask to find out if learning is happening.

4. What are some ways that you have gained feedback from children?

5. How do knowledge and application relate to each other?

9

Remember That You
Are Teaching How to Teach

"The things you have heard me say in the presence of many witnesses entrust to reliable men who will also be qualified to teach others"

—2 Tim 2:2 NIV

In the previous chapter, the focus was on making certain that factual knowledge is getting into students, that they understand it and are able to apply it in their lives. This is the very heart of teaching. However, Paul's admonition to Timothy is valid for us also. Christian teaching is only successful when at least some students pass on to others the content that they have learned. For us to be successful teachers, some of our students must become teachers. This means that an important part of teaching is modeling being a teacher. As a teacher, you are teaching how to teach. If at least some of your students do not become teachers, you have failed in your gifting as a teacher. The chain of Gospel knowledge ends with your students and you will not have achieved the larger purpose of your gifting.

You should therefore think not only about what works in a given class but also how the students in that class will reproduce the act of teaching. Nearly every teacher in the church learns what it means to be a teacher of the Gospel by having been taught in the church. This means you are teaching both facts and how to teach. Your students, whom God later gifts to the church as teachers, will imitate your approach. Sometimes this manifests itself in superficial and even amusing ways. For example, if the teacher holds her Bible in a certain way while teaching, students may unconsciously imitate the gesture. Often there is a favorite word or expression that is used repeatedly by a teacher that finds its way into the vocabulary of the students. This type of trivial reproduction is common around Bible colleges where students tend to pick up traits of favored teachers. I remember that while I was attending Bible college a certain teacher made the expression 'go butt a stump' popular. Another referred to those who held unorthodox ideas as 'Twinkies' or stated that their ideas were 'off the wall'. Over thirty years later, I still hear these words and phrases repeated by those who heard them in class.

Less obvious, but more important, is the reproduction of ideas about intentionality, techniques, and methods. For example, I was well equipped with knowledge of the Bible and theology when I began my first pastorate and understood how to preach. However, there was little going on in the way of formal church activities beyond Sunday morning worship, Sunday evening worship, and an adult Bible study on Wednesday night. The church I attended while in Bible College had a bus program, a full range of programs for children on Wednesday, and an active youth group. Without any intentionality or thought of whether it was God's plan for this church, I set out to reproduce the church I had attended. Within a few months, we had a full range of children's activities on Wednesday evenings with a bus picking up children. We started a youth group and turned it over to adult sponsors. In short, I reproduced the church I came from. I had learned one and only one way to pastor a church from the example of my previous pastor.

Without any thought or intentionality, I reproduced the way of doing church that I had experienced.

In this case, my unconscious learning by imitation worked out well. The church has continued in the model we initiated through four more pastors over a period of more than thirty years and has experienced growth. However, what if that approach had not fit that church at all? That church happened to have a large number of capable and willing adults who could lead children's activities. Adults were available for youth leaders. A little used bus was available to be put into use with a willing and able driver. However, what if none of these things had been present? I had never been taught to think intentionally about how to lead a church. I did not know that there were other models of church ministry. If the right elements had not been present, I would have been at a loss as to what to do in the church.

That was exactly the case in the second church I pastored. It did not have a bus. When it was offered a van as a gift, the church rejected the gift. It did not have a large number of capable and willing adults who could lead activities. I was at a loss as to what to do. The only model I knew did not match the circumstance I faced. The result was not very good. I had learned an approach to pastoring a church. What I had not been taught was how to think intentionally about different ways to pastor a church. Neither the pastor of the church I had attended nor the Bible College nor the seminary communicated to me that there were alternate ways to do church. The idea of thinking intentionally about which model might be best for a particular church was never even mentioned.

Today there are a variety of models for church leadership and structure being taught. Future leaders are told that they must prayerfully seek God for the best way to lead in a particular church. Unfortunately, even this current instruction seems to be mostly by books written by successful pastors rather than as a deliberate part of pastoral training. Nevertheless, because the idea is at least presented today leaders are not at a loss when the approach they are most familiar with is a poor fit for their location. Whether from class notes or the numerous books and seminars available today, leaders are aware of different models of ministry. These leaders can seek God for guidance for an approach that works where God has sent them.

Right now if you are teaching a Sunday school class or a small group you are probably saying, so what? I am not a pastor nor am I training pastors. True, but you are training witnesses, workers, and future teachers. You do not want to leave these future teachers in the situation that I found myself in as a pastor. I knew of one, and only one way to do church. If you do not somehow let them know that there is more than one way to teach a class, they will likely think that there is only way. That one way will be the way they see you teaching their class. They will look at how you teach and most of the time they will do the same thing. If they are in a situation where this approach works, it will be great. If they are not in a situation where the approach they saw you use works, they will be in trouble. This means that you need to consciously think about how the approaches you use might be reused by a future teacher. It is also critical that your students know that you are intentional about your approaches to teaching. They need to know that you are teaching the way you are teaching because they are the people that they are. They need to understand that if the class were different you would be doing things differently

Today most teachers use some kind of prepared curriculum. This will also likely be the case for the future teachers we are training. Those who write curriculum for teachers are usually intentional about the content of the lessons. Great efforts are put into making certain that the whole Bible is covered in Sunday school curriculum. Detailed plans are drawn for boys and girls groups so that important doctrines are taught at age appropriate times. However, techniques and methods for teaching the Bible and theology are often taken from lists handed out long before and focused on suburban culture. In reality there is little else they can do since they do not know your class. However, you know your class. You must choose from among their ideas and techniques what will work best for your class. You may even need to use a different technique from any that they mention. For the purpose of training future teachers, you need to mention in some way from time to time that you are not bound by techniques written in the curriculum but are using a specific technique because it fits the class. Our students who become teachers will find themselves in a variety of situations that require a variety of approaches. We must teach not only content but we must prepare future teachers by letting them know that we are not bound to what it printed in the curriculum but are using whatever techniques we think will work the best in this class.

In general terms whatever approach you are using is a class, you should from time to time say why you are using it. For example, occasionally when you show a picture, make a point to say that you are using a picture because most people are visual learners and you want to make sure that as many students as possible get something. When you draw out something on the board, you can say something similar. Simply mention you are doing it this way because it helps people to learn. I have a Roman denarius that I let people handle from time to time. I point out how small it is to actually hold and how pictures always make them seem bigger. I am not only educating people about denarii but about the value of using objects in teaching. Subtle comments while you are doing something let future teachers grasp the purpose and value of different techniques. With children, you can say to them in the course of a memory game that we are playing this game to help you to remember this information. If you use a testimony of either encouragement or warning for teens simply say what you are doing. These very brief injected remarks let the current students, and future teachers, know why you are doing something and the reason for that approach.

A very subtle example of how I have taught using an intentional approach is that I continued to use an overhead projector in some classes even after PowerPoint became available. Today everyone uses PowerPoint. If you do not use PowerPoint, people assume that you are not up to speed with the world. You are too stupid to figure out what they use all the time. However, I made a deliberative choice to stick with an overhead projector when teaching classes in certain small very rural churches. While some of these churches had acquired video projectors in the sanctuary, none were using video projectors in the classrooms. One did occasionally use their projector to show a movie to a group, though most used a DVD player and an old television. I do not know of a single instance in any of these churches where a video projector was used in Sunday school. Few, if any of the people in these churches, use a computer for presentations at work. Most do not use computers at home. At my last contact, only one of them has begun using PowerPoint as a replacement for an overhead during worship as a way to project the words to sing. On the other hand, most of these churches have several overhead projectors just sitting around since they made nice hand-me-downs from larger and more affluent churches.

If I had used a video projector and PowerPoint in these churches, it would have said to these students, "You cannot teach because you do not have a video projector or the ability to use it." However, because I used an overhead projector they could do what I did since they have plenty of overhead projectors. The projectors had transparency film stacked on top of them that could be used with or without a computer and printer. Am I saying that you should not use the newest and best approaches? No, I am not. When I teach in a college classroom, I use PowerPoint for most class sessions. In the churches where I know video projectors are in use, I use them for classes. However, I chose to use an overhead projector where that was all that was available to my students. The idea is that rather than thinking they cannot teach, they will be encouraged to use the best equipment that they have available when they teach Sunday school, boys groups, girls groups or a Bible study.

Whether you use white boards, objects, or handouts from time to time you say something about why you are using this. This can be briefly stated in clear language or very subtle. If you have people role playing something you can ask if it helps them to understand the situation better. You then can say something like role-play certainly works well with this class. In a different class, I would have had to try something else. You have just taught three things. First, you are teaching that you selected the role-play technique intentionally for this class. Second, there are different ways to teach whatever you are teaching. Third, you are telling them that a different class might require a different technique. Doing things like this requires very little effort or time but it educates and helps prepare future teachers to be intentional.

Another important part of teaching is to let the class know that you are using your toolbox. All that is required is that you mention from time to time, where you found a specific bit of information. This takes little effort and will raise your credibility with most students. It sets the example for your class and especially for any future teachers in the class you show that outside research and preparation matters. Letting the class know where you found some piece of background knowledge also lifts off you some the responsibility for the information. If someone does not like what you say, your response can always be that it did not originate with you. It is the best you could find. This also shows any future teacher in the class that they can have the same bit of insulation against criticism. What you do as a teacher the future teachers in your class will someday do as well.

A final area that you must model for future teachers is getting feedback to make certain that learning is taking place. Future teachers know when you are testing or quizzing them in some way. They get what you are doing whether it is an overt test, memory game, or just individual questions. In training future teachers, you need to say something that communicates the importance of making certain that the students have learned the material. Getting the feedback to confirm that people have learned the material always requires effort and intention. Doing it well is never easy. Consequently making certain that learning has happened is probably the easiest part of teaching to leave out. If you do not clearly communicate the importance of confirming that learning has happened, any future teacher that you have probably will not bother with the effort involved.

In conclusion, you must think long term about how your students who become teachers will imitate your example when they teach. This is why you must not only be intentional about the approaches you select for teaching approaches to any given class but you must communicate that you intentionally selected these approaches for the class in front of you. You must not only use a toolbox, you must let your students see that you use a toolbox. You must not only find ways to measure whether or not learning is taking place; you must communicate the importance of confirming that students have learned the material. When you have done this, you will have laid the foundation for effective teaching by those whom God will call and gift as teachers from among your students.

DISCUSSION QUESTIONS

1. Why is it vital that we prepare future teachers?

2. How have you communicated to your class your intentionality in using a teaching technique?

3. How have you changed your own approach to teaching in a class from what you experienced as a student?

4. What three things do you communicate when you say you chose a particular approach your class but other approaches are possible?

5. Which teacher that you sat under helped the most in preparing you to be a teacher?

10

Preparing the Lesson

AN EARLIER CHAPTER FOCUSED on intentionality in use of teaching techniques. I made a point of the differences between classes in age and background. This chapter takes the idea a step further into the actually preparation of the lesson. Before getting to the best approaches, I want to make you uncomfortable by mentioning some wrong approaches. First, 'The Expert', is someone who 'knows how to teach' and expects the students to learn. Those who think like this are often both knowledgeable and experienced. The problem is that they have exactly the same approach wherever and whenever they are in front of a class. Rather than adapting to the class, they expect the class to learn because they are teaching. This is really a display of arrogance. It will impress some classes but will not usually be very effective in actually teaching the Word of God. The second wrong approach is the teacher who knows what the class likes and always gives it to them. With adults, this may amount to reading some verses and then spending most of the time in class discussion. For children it may be the crafts' approach where a story is told briefly and then, the rest of the class is always the hand-work of the week. Preparation is straightforward and the class is happy. The third wrong approach is always going by the book. This approach is often taken by the teacher who has little or no confidence but is handed a book and told to, "Just teach the lesson". These often work quite hard to slavishly adopt whatever the book says to do. After all, the author must be an expert and the designated teacher knows he is not an expert! What this "untrained" teacher gets is a series of approaches that may have sounded good to the expert but fit neither the teacher nor his class. The problem with all three of these approaches to teaching is that real learning is not even a serious consideration.

In contrast to these fallacies, real teachers adjust presentations to the experience and background of whatever group they are teaching at a given time. This means they are flexible in the approaches that they take to teaching. Most teachers are most comfortable with one or two approaches. It is natural that as people these teachers will favor the approaches they are most comfortable using. Unfortunately, there may also be a laziness factor as some approaches to teaching require more preparation than others. Real teachers will care enough about their students to attempt to use whatever approach seems most likely to yield the best results. Teaching is ultimately about the student's learning, not the teacher's comfort. As a result real teachers will make the effort to use what seems to be the best method for presenting a particular part of the Bible to their specific group of students.

What kind of presentation is most likely to be effective with a given age group? As was discussed earlier, there are obvious differences between adults and children but there are also great differences between a five year old child and ten year old child. Most of those teaching children use a curriculum with lesson outlines. The material and techniques suggested are matched to the children's ages. They may not, however, be matched to your class. Generally adult curriculum assumes that all adults are the same. Obviously, they are not. There are often large differences between younger and older adults based on when they were in school. Public education has changed dramatically in forty years. Where people are in life will also affect their thinking. Grandparents and those with young children look at life differently. Single parents, empty-nesters and retirees all come with different mindsets. Other generational differences include how comfortable people are with technology or how open they are to different subjects or how open they are to different teaching techniques.

As a teacher you must evaluate your class and make an effort to select the best techniques for your class and the material you are teaching. Sometimes this is obvious. Maps of Paul's travels are good for just about any group when you are talking about Acts or Paul's letters. However, imagine you are talking to a husbands' or wives' group about relationships with their spouses. To make a point you tell the wives or husbands to take out their cell phones and text a specific message to their spouses. This would work well with younger groups but it is not likely to work well with a group of senior saints. Turning things around, imagine trying to set up a twenty-four hour prayer chain when the class is mostly two job households with small children at home. Both of these are extreme examples; but, teachers need to pay attention to less obvious differences as well.

An issue of similar effect is the academic and employment background of a specific group of students. Several years ago I failed in a leadership training class when I asked the students to create a teaching outline from an assigned Bible passage. I thought this would be easy. It was easy for the half of the class that had college degrees and white-collar jobs. These students read their passages and had their outlines ready to discuss in under five minutes. One man who changed tires for a living had not yet finished reading his passage when the woman next to him showed that she had finished an outline. My failure to properly evaluate the class and adjust the lesson to include everyone had real life consequences. The man was so discouraged he never took another class.

Teaching often emphasizes classroom skills. It tends to favor the already well educated and those who handle paperwork in some form. However, we must always remember we are teaching the Word of God which is intended to change lives and affect behavior of everyone. The ability to grasp and manipulate information quickly is a strong advantage in most classroom situations. However, our goals in teaching the Word of God include not just knowledge but also understanding and application. The advantages of the academically astute apply primarily to the acquisition of knowledge. They may or may not help with understanding or with application in a person's life.

The culture and experience of those living in biblical times have little to do with our modern information economy. A white-collar worker is at a distinct disadvantage in understanding many of the situations described in the Bible. Imagine someone who grew up in a city and now works as a receptionist in an office. Now imagine someone who grew up in the country and has cared for livestock all her life. The country person has been up at all hours and out in all kinds of weather to take care of the animals. If you are teaching from a passage that speaks of David as a shepherd or even speaks of the Lord as shepherd. The country person has an inherent advantage in comprehension. Those who know nothing of the monotony of taking care of stock punctuated with the sudden need to find a missing animal or to 'pull a lamb' may never grasp the meaning. For pure city dwellers getting the meaning of 'shepherd' across may take multiple approaches and illustrations. In addition someone with experience taking care of livestock will much more quickly understand not just the words but the meaning of these kinds of passages. Part of being a teacher means that with God's help we must consider both the material and the background of the class and then prepare the lesson with the techniques that seem most likely to produce learning in the students who are entrusted to us.

It sometimes helps to think about how truth is presented in the Bible. Essentially, there are three approaches: propositional truth, narrative truth, and metaphoric truth. A propositional truth is a statement that affirms, denies, or commands something. For example, 'God is Love' is a statement about God. 'Blessed are the merciful for they shall obtain mercy' is another example. Propositional truth is in essence a principle stated directly in Scripture. Biblically, a narrative is a true story told to teach a principle. The stories of Noah and the ark, David and Saul, and Jesus' baptism are all examples of narrative truth. Metaphoric truth is truth presented symbolically. The range of metaphoric truth is very broad: including the Old Testament sacrifices, parables, God clothing the flowers beautifully, Jeremiah smashing a pot, and much of the content of dreams and visions. You must find the intended truth in the metaphor. That truth is the principle your class needs to learn.

The question is what teaching technique is the best choice for teaching these truths to your class. For a propositional truth, you could post the statement in your room and refer to it often. You could have everyone say it aloud together repeatedly. You could write it on the board and read it together removing a word each time. You could have your class say it aloud together when a key phrase is used. You could lead a discussion about how this truth applies to our lives. What you are looking for is the best technique for presenting the truth to your class and having the class understand it and be able to apply it in their lives.

Narrative truth is basically a story. Stories can be told with pictures or even video. Class members can act out stories. You, the teacher, can act out the story as you tell it. As the teacher, you have to figure out what technique will best teach the material to your class and facilitate their understanding of the story. It may well be a combination of techniques. After telling the story, you might ask questions about the story itself to see if people followed the content. You could ask the class what the story means. For small children you might have them make something suggested by the story. The narrative is what you are teaching; the technique is how you are teaching it.

Metaphoric truth is somewhat like an illustration in a sermon. It is designed to be a window that lets in the light. The difficulty is that the window was designed for another time and another culture. What might have been a crystal clear window in Israel 2800 years ago is fogged over for a modern audience. This means that metaphoric truths often require extra explanation. At the same time, metaphoric truth comes in so many different forms it has unique opportunities for presentation. For example, you could smash a pot like Jeremiah. The key would be making sure your class understood what smashing the pot meant. Pictures are frequently very helpful when dealing with metaphoric truth. Smaller children will usually need visual representations of metaphoric truths in order to understand them. The key is making sure that whatever technique or techniques you use make the meaning clear to your class. You do not want to hang an opaque curtain over an already fogged window.

Whatever approach to teaching you take, remember that you are teaching principles. Many propositional statements are already principles. For those that are not, you must find the underlying principle and present it in some form. You must generally find the principle for narrative and metaphoric truth. This is not a lesson sidelight. The underlying principle is what the story or metaphor is teaching. It is therefore what you should be teaching. Many passages have multiple principles embedded in them. You must ask God for guidance and generally focus on one principle for your class.

Once you have settled on what principle is going to be the focus of the lesson, teaching that principle will guide the rest of the preparation for the class. Your goals for the lesson become your class knowing the content, understanding what the passage means, and then applying the principle contained in the passage in their lives. These goals give you filters to think about what techniques are the best choices for your class at each stage of this process. Breaking down the lesson into these three goals can make preparation much easier. For each goal you consider different approaches, evaluate your class's learning, and either move forward or re-teach the material.

Sometimes narrative truths or metaphoric truths are combined with propositional truths. In these cases the propositional truth is usually the main principle being taught and the metaphoric or narrative truth is an illustration of the principle. Jesus uses the narrative of Noah and the Ark to illustrate His proposition, "Therefore keep watch, because you do not know on what day your Lord will come." Matt 24:42 NIV Sometimes Jesus puts a proposition and metaphor together so closely it is easy to miss what He is doing. In Matt 7:15 Jesus warns of false prophets. "Watch out for false prophets. They come to you in sheep's clothing, but inwardly they are ferocious wolves". NIV The first sentence is the proposition. The second sentence illustrates the proposition with one of the most familiar metaphors in the Bible, a wolf in sheep's clothing. In Luke 10 Jesus uses the story of the Good Samaritan to illustrate the proposition, "Love your neighbor as yourself". Luke 10:27 NIV You can do the same kind of things as you work with principles.

As you are wrestling with what principle to focus on and techniques to use in a particular class remember that you are placed in position of being a teacher by God. You are not alone; the Holy Spirit is with you to guide you and God has gifted you to do the work. Therefore you should be praying though out the time you are preparing. After you pray, you should spend some time listening. You will be amazed how the Spirit will guide you to focus a specific principle that is exactly what someone needed. It can be even more amazing when you ask for help to see how the Spirit will guide you into approaches that work. It is therefore best to start working on a lesson early. Then you have time to pray about what principles to focus on and how to best present the material to your class. During this time be sensitive to God leading you into what He wants done. After all, you have been called and gifted by God for this work.

DISCUSSION QUESTIONS

1. Which of the three wrong approaches discussed at the beginning of this lesson tempts you the most?

2. Describe the background of your students. How does this affect how you teach?

3. What three ways does the Bible present truth?

4. Read Jer 19:10–11. What is the principle behind the metaphor? How would you teach this to your class?

5. What is the difference between principles and illustrations?

11

Four Concluding Issues

PREPARED TEACHERS SHOULD SPEAK WITH CONFIDENCE

TEACHERS WHO HAVE PREPARED well and understand that God has gifted them for the work of teaching should speak with confidence and boldness. In this we have the example of Jesus who, when He taught, spoke with confidence. "When Jesus had finished saying these things, the crowds were amazed at his teaching, 29 because he taught as one who had authority, and not as their teachers of the law." Matt 7:28–29 NIV Many current teachers will respond by saying that of course Jesus spoke with confidence; He is the Son of God! I am just me, with plenty of faults and failings. Both of these statements are certainly true. But Jesus is also fully man and Heb 4:15 reminds us that He well understood the weakness of being a man. That is at least part of why the man Jesus prepared for His ministry by studying at the synagogue at least weekly for most of 30 years. Luke 2 also tells of Him as an adolescent making use of an opportunity to interact with the teachers of the Law in Jerusalem. Jesus did not just teach from His knowledge as the Son of God but He prepared as the Son of Man.

The Holy Spirit gifted the man Jesus at the time of His baptism by John to carry out His ministry. Put another way, the Father placed the Holy Spirit on Jesus to empower Him to carry out His work. This means that Jesus did this work as a man gifted by God for the purpose and not in His power as the Second Person of the Trinity. This must include His work of teaching. In the same way, those gifted by God as teachers for the church are empowered by God through that gift to be effective. The idea is that just as Jesus was gifted by God to do His work of teaching you are also gifted by God for the work of teaching. You can therefore teach in the same kind of giftedness as Christ. The same God who empowered Jesus for teaching also empowers you for teaching. This means as you prepare for teaching and trust God for effectiveness in teaching you can teach with confidence on the same basis that Jesus taught with confidence.

When you know your material well and speak about it confidently, people often attribute great weight to your words. This places on teachers a great responsibility. If you are correct, you will influence many people for eternal good. However, if you are teaching error you may lead men to eternal damnation. This is why Jas 3:1 warns us that teachers will face a stricter judgment. If someone sits in the back pew and silently believes a deadly heresy, they may miss heaven. However, they will not necessarily take others with them to hell. If a teacher promotes false doctrine, they will likely persuade others to believe it also. The result will be many people suffering possibly for all eternity. As teachers, we must therefore take care that what we confidently affirm agrees with the Word of God. By teaching, we can do great harm or we can be a great blessing. Let us be diligent that we are a blessing in the church helping to advance God's kingdom.

PASTORS SHOULD REMEMBER THAT TEACHERS ARE A GIFT FROM GOD

All of the gifts mentioned by Paul in Romans 12 are vital to the health of any church. Churches lacking believers with these gifts must limp along trying to fill the gaps and praying that God will provide for the need among them. The focus of this book has been on those gifted as teachers. Very effective teachers occasionally intimidate pastors who lack confidence because those with the gift of teaching also interpret the Bible and give doctrinal understanding to other believers. This is understandable, but a grave mistake. No pastor could possibly do all the teaching in all the places that these God gifted teachers do in the church. When God has blessed a church with multiple teachers, He has prepared that church for success.

Therefore, pastors should rejoice when they have multiple God – gifted teachers in their church. By teaching in small groups scattered across the church, teachers are helping pastors by doing work the pastors cannot do themselves. The work of teaching and the work of discipleship are vital to the health of any church. Yet, no pastor can provide this in a small group setting to more than a small portion of a church. But, collectively, that is exactly what teachers do for the church. In addition, by building relationships in small groups they provide cohesion to the church as a whole that cannot be achieved in any other way. They become aware of struggles and questions that people are dealing with and can address these issues when they are small. What clear thinking pastor is not delighted when they have help with the hard and consuming work of discipleship? Pastors should also consider that the teachers who work with children probably are responsible for more people coming to salvation than anyone else in the church. In this world, teachers of children are generally unsung and rarely honored; but, heaven is rejoicing and pastors should be as well.

Pastors should consequently recognize that God – gifted teachers are complimentary to the office of pastor that they have been called to fill. Consequently, they should honor and celebrate teachers before the church. While we always must work for the glory of God rather than the applause of men, no one wants to serve week after week and year after year without acknowledgement. Just as pastors may have hours of unseen work behind a sermon in the same way there are often hours of unseen work behind a lesson taught to a small group. When pastors preach an outstanding sermon they are often able to bask in appreciation afterwards. This is rarely the case for teachers no matter how much work goes into a class. Wise pastors will show appreciation to all those who serve in the Romans 12 gifts and especially those who make the commitment to teach and do the behind the scenes work to be highly effective in the work.

PASTORS AND CHURCHES SHOULD SHOW APPRECIATION TO TEACHERS

A good way to show teachers that they are valued is by providing practical help to them in their work. This is not a substitute for the occasional expression of appreciation from the front of the church or a recognition dinner but an additional action. Pastors often have the opportunity to attend seminars or receive training from others who are highly successful in the work of church leadership. Wise pastors and churches make use of these opportunities. Teachers who provide a major part of the work of teaching and discipleship in the church can benefit from similar opportunities. Some churches have the resources to provide this kind of opportunity in house by bringing in trainers. Churches with fewer resources may need to join with others to provide such opportunities. Often denominations will provide training opportunities in area or statewide meetings. All of these training opportunities take time and most cost money. No church has an unlimited supply of either. However, in deciding how to invest resources, church leaders should consider the collective value provided to the church by the teachers in the small groups of the church.

Another way to both honor and help these teachers is to provide them study resources. This costs some money but no time to the church as a whole. A book or two a year can make a large cumulative difference for diligent teachers trying to fill their toolboxes. This applies both to those working with adults and to those working with children. A book explaining a hundred games that can be played in a confined area may have uncountable value to a teacher of ten year old boys. Providing a gift certificate to Christianbook.com or a similar website with the understanding that it will be used to purchase study resources is a great gesture. When it is presented to teachers as a way of expressing appreciation in front of the church as a whole it can have a double value.

A practical, if intangible benefit, of this kind of support is to lessen the dependence of many teachers on websites of dubious value. Printed resources from established publishers are typical vetted for general accuracy. By getting good material into the hands of those who do most of the teaching with the least formal preparation, churches are paving the way for the best outcomes. Someone will ask, why not build a strong church library? That way more resources can be made available to more of the teachers and if some teacher quits the money spent on books for them will not be wasted. The answer is simple; most of those teaching prepare their lessons at home. They will only rarely have time to come to the church at an off time and use the resources stored in a church's library. When people make time to prepare they use the tools they have on hand. If teachers have helpful material available at home it benefits the whole church.

WHAT ABOUT FALSE TEACHERS

Most experienced pastors and many other church leaders will have one or more horror stories about some teacher in a church that caused trouble, friction, and even divisions. These things happen because of sin, placing someone where they are not gifted, personality conflicts, or other administrative causes. But they do not necessarily mean that the teacher involved is a false teacher. False teachers are not those with whom you have a disagreement, but those who teach false doctrines. There is no shortage of false teachers in the New Testament from end to end. Jesus warned of the disciples against the teaching of the Pharisees and Sadducees in Matt 16:12. The former held to an external form of salvation based in legalism and the latter rejected the idea of angels, spirits, the resurrection, and all but the books of Moses. Paul speaks of

Hymenaeus and Philetus in 2 Tim 2:17 who were teaching that the resurrection had already taken place. The Spirit in Rev 2:20 warns the church in Thyatira of Jezebel who was teaching the acceptance of sexual immorality. The point is that false teachers are not those who we find annoying or who teach something we disagree with. False teachers are those teaching false doctrines that will ultimately rob people of their salvation.

Again it is vital to realize that none of these doctrines I mentioned in the last paragraph are minor disagreements. All of them are spoken of as beliefs that would separate a person from God and bring eternal condemnation. In contrast, believers disagreed over eating meat offered to idols, having a special day to worship, and vegetarianism. A vegetarian confronted with another believer eating a bloody steak that originated in a pagan temple is going to have a hard time calling them brother. Someone who insists that Sunday morning is special will not be happy with someone who works every Sunday and worships on Tuesday evening. Yet in Romans 14 Paul tells them to get along with one another and leave the rest to God. The conclusion is that we should not condemn someone as a false teacher over issues that are not at the core of the faith. In modern terms we may hold a pretribulation, mid-tribulation, post-tribulation or even amillennial position on Christ's return but we better all agree that there will be a resurrection and judgment. This does not mean that everyone can fit into every local church. For the sake of peace, if someone, including a teacher, holds beliefs significantly different from their local church they may need to find another local church more in line with their positions.

When someone within the church is teaching false doctrines that contradict truths that are central to the Gospel there are clear instructions for dealing with them. First those in charge should simply order them to stop. Paul instructs Timothy about this when Timothy was leading the church in Ephesus. "As I urged you when I went into Macedonia, stay there in Ephesus so that you may command certain men not to teach false doctrines any longer" 1 Tim 1:3 NIV The hope is that they will stop teaching whatever falsehoods in which they have been caught. If someone rejects multiple warnings to stop Paul gave instruction in Titus 3:10 to have nothing more to do with them. That is, they should be ejected from the church. On a practical level, the ejection of someone from the church does not mean that they disappear from the community. Unfortunately they often remain nearby and seek to draw away weak believers after them. Therefore one qualification given for pastors in Titus 1:9 is that they are able to refute false doctrines. The sin of false doctrine will continue until the end and church leadership must deal with it just as any other sin. Nevertheless we must be careful to distinguish false teachers from those we merely find annoying or with whom we have peripheral disagreements.

DISCUSSION QUESTIONS

1. What allows teachers to speak with confidence?

2. How can a very effective teacher reassure a pastor who is worried that the teacher might usurp their position?

3. How have you been shown appreciation by the church for your work of teaching?

4. How would you like to be shown appreciation by the church for your work of teaching?

5. Define the term false teacher

Bibliography

Barna, George, *Transforming Children into Spiritual Champions*. Ventura, California: Regal, 2003.

Lovett, C. S., *Soul Winning is Easy*. Grand Rapids: Zondervan, 1957.